Illustrated
Word Smart

A Visual Vocabulary Builder

The Princeton Review

Illustrated
Word Smart

A Visual Vocabulary Builder

Tom Meltzer

Illustrations by Lisa Vingleman

Random House, Inc.
New York

www.PrincetonReview.com

Princeton Review Publishing, L.L.C.
2315 Broadway
New York, NY   10024
Email: booksupport@review.com
Copyright ©1999 by Princeton Review Publishing, L.L.C.

ISBN   0-375-75189-0

Editor: Lesly Atlas
Production Editor: Kristen Azzara
Production: Saucy Enterprizes

9   8   7

ACKNOWLEDGMENTS

First and foremost, thanks to The Princeton Review, especially Evan Schnittman and John Katzman, for giving us the opportunity to work on this exciting and fun project and for having faith that we could get it done despite all evidence indicating the reasonableness of a contrary conclusion. Thanks also to our editor, Lesly Atlas, for her patience and guidance.

Thanks to Judy Vingleman, Daryle Vingleman, and Judy Meltzer for their love and support. Thanks also to Scott Murphy for kicking Lisa in the butt occasionally. Finally, thanks to Matthew Licht and Dian Hanson for inspiration.

CONTENTS

INTRODUCTION

Let's face it: rote memorization is boring. And difficult. And inefficient. How many times have you sat down to commit something to memory—multiplication tables, musical scales, rules and vocabulary for a foreign language, the periodic table—only to walk away hours later confused, frustrated, and none the wiser for the effort?

The first two books in this series, *Word Smart* and *Word Smart II*, set out to make the memorization of vocabulary easier by making it more fun. This book, *Illustrated Word Smart*, takes those efforts one step further. Our goal in this book is to present the 250 words that appear most frequently on the difficult portions of the SAT—and have thus earned the imprimatur of "important words" from the esteemed Educational Testing Service—in a way that would make it *impossible* for you to forget them.

Here's what we did: for each of the 250 words in this book, we came up with a mnemonic device. A *mnemonic device* is anything that aids in memory. In this book, we use rhymes, words, and phrases that are similar to the vocabulary word, and other techniques to help you remember. Take a look at the following example:

---

abstruse

definition: difficult to understand (adjective)

mnemonic: I'M ABSOLUTELY TRULY CONFUSED.

As you can see, the word *abstruse* can be found in the phrase "I'm absolutely truly confused," which also conveys the very meaning of the word.

Here's another:

---

replete

definition: full; abundantly supplied (adjective)

mnemonic: I EAT AND EAT 'TIL I'M REPLETE

In this case, the mnemonic device is a rhyme to help you remember the meaning of *replete*.

As an extra helpful tool, where applicable, we have provided icons so you can easily determine which mnemonics are visual and which are auditory. Many are both visual and auditory.

LOOKS LIKE

SOUNDS LIKE

Finally, we added a humorous illustration to reinforce the mnemonic device. The illustration and the mnemonic device provide two extra means of learning each vocabulary word beyond memorizing its definition. The end result, we hope, is a book that is both useful and entertaining. Students preparing for the SAT should find it particularly helpful, but it should also be useful to adults who hope to expand their vocabulary.

HOW TO USE THIS BOOK

This book is divided into seventeen chapters of thematically related words. One chapter covers words typically used to describe emotions; another presents words often used in reference to the arts; and so on. Each chapter offers a bite-sized vocabulary list, suitable for digestion in one sitting. Seventeen sessions with *Illustrated Word Smart*, we hope, should be enough to improve your vocabulary dramatically. Have fun testing your newfound knowledge with the challenging puzzles at the back of this book.

Don't try to memorize all the words in this book in one sitting. You need to give yourself time to process each list of words, to allow it to transfer from your short-term memory—which you use while you are studying—to your long-term memory, the more permanent storehouse of knowledge and experiences. Plan to study two or three of these chapters each week, until you have worked your way through the entire book.

PRONUNCIATION

We don't use standard dictionary phonetics in our *Word Smart* books for the simple reason that many people don't understand them. Instead, we use a modified phonetic approach that we believe is largely intuitive. The pronunciation key below should clear up any questions you might have about how to use our pronunciation guide:

The letter(s)	*is (are) pronounced like the letter(s)*	*in the word(s)*
a	a	bat, can
ah	o	con, on
aw	aw	paw, straw
ay	a	skate, rake
e	e	stem, hem, err
ee	ea	steam, clean
i	i	rim, chin, hint
ing	ing	sing, ring
oh	o	row, tow
oo	oo	room, boom
ow	ow	cow, brow
oy	oy	boy, toy
u, uh	u	run, bun
y (ye, eye)	i	climb, time
ch	ch	chair, chin
f	f, ph	film, phony
g	g	go, goon
j	j	join, jungle
k	c	cool, cat
s	s	solid, wisp
sh	sh	shoe, wish
z	z	zoo, razor
zh	s	measure

All other consonants are pronounced as you would expect. Capitalized letters are accented.

PUT IN A GOOD WORD:

Words Describing Positive Attributes or Actions

affable (AF uh bul)

easy-going; friendly *(adjective)*

 AFFECTION-ABLE

The word *affable* derives from the Latin word meaning "to speak to." This makes sense, because an *affable* person is easy to speak to. *Ineffable*, meaning "indescribable," stems from the same root.

amenable (uh MEEN uh bul)

favorably disposed; willing to change *(adjective)*

 AMENDABLE

Synonyms for *amenable* include responsive, receptive, and acquiescent. Antonyms include closed-minded, obstinate, and recalcitrant.

amiable (AY mee uh bul)

good-natured and likable *(adjective)*

MON AMI or AMIGO

The Latin word for "friend" is *amicus*. It is the root for the French word *ami* (meaning "friend"), the Spanish word *amigo* (meaning "friend"), and the English words *amiable*, *amicable* (both meaning "friendly") and *amity* (meaning "friendship").

apt (APT)

suitable; appropriate *(adjective)*

APPROPRIATE

The word *apt* implies that something is not only appropriate but also to the point. An *apt* comment is more likely to be terse than florid.

assiduous (uh SIJ oo us)

hard-working *(adjective)*

 ASS IN THE DUST

The word *assiduous* implies persistence, as in the hard-working ass pictured above. One might say, "Bill made *assiduous* efforts to improve his free throws, shooting from the foul line for an hour every night."

benevolent (buh NEV uh lunt)

kind; generous (*adjective*)

 BEN IS nEVer viOLENT (SEE BEN THE HIPPY)

The word *benevolent* combines the Latin word *bene*, meaning "well," and *volens*, meaning "to wish." Its literal meaning: to wish well. The root *bene* also appears in *benefit* and *benefactor*.

camaraderie (kah muh RA duh ree)

good will between friends *(noun)*

COMRADES, YOU AND ME

Both the words *camaraderie* and *comrade* are derived from the same Latin word, meaning "roommate." If there is no *camaraderie* between you and your roommate, it is time to find a new one!

conscientious (kon shee EN shus)

careful and thorough in work; guided by conscience and good moral sense *(adjective)*

CONSCIENCE SENT US

You might have heard the term *conscientious objector*. It refers to a person who refuses to serve in the military, for either religious or moral reasons.

cordial (KOR-juhl)

warm and sincere; friendly *(adjective)*

 CORD + DIAL

The English word *cordial* comes from the Latin word meaning "heart." A *cordial* action demonstrates that a person has a big heart.

decorous (DEK uhr us)

proper; marked by good taste (*adjective*)

 DECent and cOuRteOUS

A person who is *decorous* is said to exhibit proper behavior, or *decorum*.

diligent (DIL uh jint)

hard-working; persevering and painstaking (*adjective*)

 BEING TOO DILIGENT CAN KILL A GENT

The word *diligent* derives from the Latin word meaning "to honor and love," probably because we work most *diligently* on those projects we love.

exemplar (ig ZEM plar)

one who is worthy of imitation; an ideal model *(noun)*

EXAMPLe + stAR

Although the word *exemplar* most often refers to something or someone that is worthy of imitation, it is also occasionally used to describe something that is simply a very good example of its type.

gregarious (gri GAR ee us)

sociable and outgoing; enjoying the company of others *(adjective)*

 GREet, GAb, AND TELL RIOtoUS STORIES

The word *gregarious* derives from the Latin word meaning "the herd." A *gregarious* person is one who mixes well with the herd (of people, of course!). Other words sharing the same root include *congregation* and *segregate*.

laudatory (LAW duh tor ee)

expressing great praise *(adjective)*

 APPLAUD A STORY

The word *laudatory* derives from the Latin word meaning "to praise." Other words sharing the same root include *applaud* and *allow*. A student who has excelled in college may graduate magna cum laude (with high honors) or summa cum laude (with the greatest honors).

propriety (pro PRY uh tee)

appropriateness of behavior; the state of exhibiting proper etiquette *(noun)*

 PROPeR In sociETY

The word *propriety* often refers to the rules of proper behavior among members of high society. Protocol, by contrast, refers to the rules of proper behavior among diplomats.

prudent (PROO dint)

exercising good judgment and common sense *(adjective)*

 PRoud stUDENT

The Latin word *prudens*, meaning "wisdom" or "knowledge," is the etymological antecedent of *prudent*. Another English word with the same Latin root is *jurisprudence* (the philosophy or science of law).

sanguine (sang GWIN)

optimistic; cheerfully confident *(adjective)*

🖐 SHE SANG WE WILL WIN

The French word for "blood" is *sang*. In Medieval times, people believed that four bodily fluids, called humors, controlled an individual's health and attitude. Those in whom blood predominated were considered healthy and confident. This is how *sanguine* came to mean "optimistic." By the way, the other humors are bile, phlegm, and black bile.

DRILLS

CHAPTER 1

I. Match the word in the left-hand column with the word or phrase in the right-hand column that is most similar in meaning.

1. amenable
2. apt
3. decorous
4. exemplar
5. gregarious
6. laudatory
7. prudent
8. sanguine

a. wise
b. full of praise
c. propriety
d. agreeable
e. worthy of imitation
f. appropriate
g. optimistic
h. outgoing

II. Choose the word that best completes the meaning of the sentence.

9. Floyd's $100 donation to the local soup kitchen was a truly _benevolent_ act.
   a. indigenous
   b. benevolent
   c. specious
   d. dilatory

10. The _camaraderie_ among the four boys is so strong that one boy rarely ever does anything without the other three.
    a. austerity
    b. bias
    c. camaraderie
    d. disdain

III. Select the best answer.

11. Which word would NOT be used to describe a friendly person?

    a. amiable
    b. affable
    c. haughty
    d. cordial

12. Which word would be LEAST appropriate in a description of a hard-working person?

    a. assiduous
    b. indolent
    c. diligent
    d. conscientious

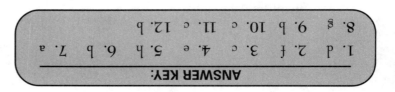

ANSWER KEY:

1. d 2. f 3. c 4. e 5. h 6. b 7. a
8. g 9. b 10. c 11. c 12. b

EXPRESS YOURSELF:
Words Describing Emotions

abhor (ab HOR)

to hate intensely *(verb)*

  ABsolutely HORrible

The word *abhor* combines the prefix ab–, meaning "away from," and the Latin word meaning "to bristle" or "to shudder." It is a particularly appropriate word to use, then, when describing things one dislikes so much that the dislike elicits physical revulsion.

diffident (DIF uh dent)

lacking confidence; quiet and shy *(adjective)*

 DIFFICULTY BEING CONF**IDENT**

All *diffident* people are shy, but not all shy people are diffident. Shyness has many possible causes; diffidence is always caused by a lack of self-confidence.

ebullience (ih BOOL yuhns)

intense and joyful enthusiasm *(noun)*

SEE JULIE DANCE

The Latin root of *ebullience* is *bullire*, meaning "to bubble." Other words sharing this root: *boil*, *bouillon* (a broth made by simmering meat in water), and *bouillabaisse* (a French seafood stew).

effusive (ih FYOO siv)

gushy; highly emotional, especially in expressing gratitude or praise *(adjective)*

HE FUSSES VERY MUCH

The word *effusive* combines the prefix e- (meaning "out from") and the Latin word meaning "to pour." Praise "pours out from" an *effusive* individual.

enervate (EN uhr vayt)

to weaken the strength or health of (verb)

DEGENERATE

The word *enervate* also has a specific medical meaning. It is the act of removing a nerve or a part of a nerve. A root canal operation, for example, is an *enervation*.

frenetic (fruh NET ik)

wildly excited or active *(adjective)*

 FRENzied + hEcTIC

The word *frenetic* derives from the ancient Greek word for "having a diseased mind." Apparently, extreme activity was once considered an indicator of mental imbalance.

impetuous (im PECH oo us)

characterized by sudden energy and emotion; impulsive and passionate *(adjective)*

IMPULSE GETS TO US

The word *impetuous* is often used to describe actions that demonstrate both impulsiveness and impatience. *Impetuous* people act quickly because they cannot stand to wait, often failing to consider all of their options.

implacable (im PLAK uh bul)

impossible to appease or satisfy *(adjective)*

 IMPossibLe TO MAKE peACeABLE

The root of *implacable* is the Latin word meaning "to calm or soothe." The word *placate*, meaning "to please," shares the same root.

listless (LIST lis)

indifferent; unwilling to act or even move; lazy *(adjective)*

  WISH LIST-LESS

In Middle English, the word for "desire" is *liste*. The literal meaning of *listless* is "without desire."

mercurial (muhr KYOOR ee uhl)

subject to rapid and extreme changes in mood; volatile *(adjective)*

FROM MERCIFUL TO FURIOUS

The word *mercurial* derives from the name of the messenger god Mercury, who was noted for his swiftness. A *mercurial* person changes moods as quickly as Mercury could run.

rancorous (RAN kor us)

hateful; marked by deep-seated ill will *(adjective)*

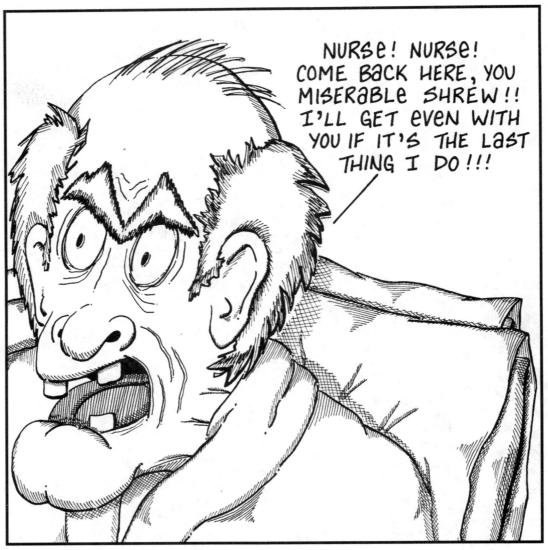

ANGER PLUS

Rancorous hatred is characterized by profound long-term anger, often over a perceived injustice. Those who hold grudges are *rancorous* individuals.

reticent (REH tih sunt)

reluctant to speak; shy *(adjective)*

RETIRING + SILENT

A *reticent* person is not merely quiet, but also is reluctant to speak, especially about personal matters. The word is often used to describe those who fear that, by speaking, they will reveal embarrassing information about themselves.

staid (STAYD)

characterized by a strait-laced sense of correct behavior;
unusually preoccupied with one's own dignity *(adjective)*

STRAIT-LACED

Some synonyms for *staid* include somber, solemn, demure, and sober-sided. Antonyms include exuberant, jaunty, playful, and capricious.

stoic (STOH ik)

indifferent to emotions or pain *(adjective)*;
one who is indifferent to emotions or pain *(noun)*

  STOny and ICy

The original Stoics were a group of Greek philosophers. They believed that all human events are preordained by Fate. Since people are unable to change their fate, they reasoned, complaining and suffering are a mere waste of time. Accordingly, the Stoics tried to accept life's ups and downs without emotion.

swagger (SWAG ur)

to boast; to strut or otherwise demonstrate excessive pride *(verb)*

 SWAying braGGER

The word *swagger* probably derives from the British verb *swag*, which means "to lurch" or "to sway" When people *swagger*, often they sway from one side to another.

tepid (TEH pid)

lukewarm; lacking emotion *(adjective)*

👁✋ TEMPERATURE IS MIDDLING

The word *tepid* is used to describe the temperature of food and liquids (e.g., "a *tepid* cup of coffee"). It is also used to describe attitudes (e.g., "he offered the candidate only *tepid* support") and emotions (e.g., "a *tepid* kiss").

torpor (TOR puhr)

laziness; inactivity; dullness (noun)

 TORPedoed vigOR

The word *torpor* derives from the Latin word meaning "to be stiff," probably because bodies grow stiff from inactivity.

trepidation (trep ih DAY shun)

uncertainty; fear *(noun)*

THUMP!
THUMP!
THUMP!
THUMP!
THUMP!

RAPID PALPITATION

The word *trepidation* derives from the Latin word meaning "to be anxious." Another word with this root is *intrepid*, which means "fearless."

wary (WEHR ee)

on guard; watchful *(adjective)*

WORRY AND SCARY

Some synonyms for *wary* include chary, suspicious, and vigilant. Antonyms include rash, foolhardy, and careless.

DRILLS

CHAPTER 2

I. Each sentence in the left-hand column gives expression to an emotion or emotional state. Match each sentence with the word in the right-hand column describing that emotion.

1. I love you! No, on second thought, I hate you!   a. tepid

2. I love you so, so much!!!!   b. effusive

3. I don't like anything, and I never will.   c. mercurial

4. I really hate you! A lot!   d. impetuous

5. I have no emotions. I am Spock.   e. implacable

6. That's a nice car. I'm going to buy it right now!   f. abhor

7. I just don't have any strong feelings on the subject.   g. stoic

II. Choose the word that best completes the meaning of the sentence.

8. The pace of the soccer game was _____; each team scored often and the lead changed hands frequently.
   a. malevolent
   b. exculpatory
   c. caustic
   d. frenetic

9. Sheila was _____ of the stray dog in her backyard and was afraid that it might bite her.
   a. wary
   b. parodic
   c. gratuitous
   d. intrepid

10. Art was more than just happy, he was downright _____.

    a. misanthropic

    b. ebullient

    c. pugnacious

    d. indolent

11. Scott lay on the couch for days, idly enjoying his state of _____.

    a. affability

    b. ingratitude

    c. torpor

    d. jurisprudence

12. Karen felt extremely _____ when she was passed up for a promotion she had worked very hard to achieve.

    a. rancorous

    b. wary

    c. ebullient

    d. impetuous

III. Select the best answer.

13. Which word would NOT be used to describe a shy person?

    a. staid

    b. diffident

    c. garrulous

    d. reticent

14. Which word would LEAST likely be used to describe an inactive person?

    a. enervated

    b. feral

    c. listless

    d. torpor

15. Karla was full of _____ at the mere thought of flying in an airplane.
    a. enmity
    b. opluence
    c. clarity
    d. trepidation

THE SPOKEN WORD:
Words Relating to Conversation

Proverb

adage (AD ij)

a wise old saying *(noun)*

A PENNY SAVED IS A PENNY EARNED! WASTE NOT, WANT NOT! MONEY DOESN'T GROW ON TREES, YOU KNOW!

 DAD THE SAGE

In Shakespeare's *Hamlet*, Polonius advises his son Laertes: "Neither a borrower nor a lender be." This quote proves that dads have been spouting *adages* for a long, long time.

Headstrong

adamant (AD uh munt)

extremely stubborn *(adjective)*

 # AD MAN'S RANT IS FORCEFUL

The word *adamant* is also the name of a stone that is harder than a diamond and was once believed to be entirely impenetrable.

Curt

brusque (BRUSK)

describing a rude, abrupt manner *(adjective)*

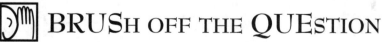 BRUSh OFF THE QUEstion

Another mnemonic device: *brusque* sounds like "big rush." Someone who is *brusque* is usually in a big rush.

aboveboard

candor (KAN dor)

sincerity; openness *(noun)*

👁 CAN stanD ON HIS wORd

The word *candor* derives from the Latin word meaning "to shine," indicating the high regard with which the Romans regarded honest people. Other words sharing the same root include *candle*, *candid*, and *incandescent*.

cavil (KAV uhl)

to raise trivial objections; to nitpick *(verb)*

 CALL IT VILE

Some synonyms for *cavil* include quibble, deprecate, belittle, and criticize. Antonyms include praise, applaud, compliment, and flatter.

(convincing)

compelling (kum PEL ing)

forceful and convincing *(adjective)*

👁 COMPANY tELLING EMPLOYEE

The word *compelling* derives from the Latin word meaning "to drive." This makes sense, because a *compelling* argument could drive your actions or choices. Other words sharing the same root include *propel, expel, repel,* and *pulsate.*

didactic (dye DAK tik)

intended to instruct *(adjective)*

  DID ACT LIKE A TEACHER

The word *didactic* comes from the Greek word meaning "to teach." People who teach themselves are called autodidacts.

disparage (di SPAR ij)

to speak of in a negative way; to belittle (verb)

DIS + SPAR + RAGE

The word *disparage* originated from a French word that was used to describe someone whose social status had been reduced by marrying into a lower class. It later took on the more general meaning "to belittle" or "to reduce the stature of."

emphatic (em FAT ik)

expressed with forceful speech *(adjective)*

 EMPHAsize TwICe

The word *emphatic* shares a Greek root with *emphasize* and *emphasis*. To be *emphatic* is to place great stress on what you are saying.

facetious (fuh SEE shus)

playfully humorous (*adjective*)

 FACE TIps yOU off, perhapS with a wink

The word *facetious* is one of very few English words in which each vowel appears exactly once and in alphabetical order.

Candid

frank (FRANK)

open and sincere in expression; straightforward *(adjective)*

THANK FRANK FOR HIS HONESTY

The word *frank* is sometimes used to describe someone who is too straightforward to the point of tactlessness. The wiener in the illustration, for example, is certainly expressing his opinion *frankly*, but could perhaps use a lesson in manners.

fulminate (FUL muh nayt)

to denounce loudly and forcefully; to explode *(verb)*

FULL OF MENACE

The word *fulminate* derives from the Latin word meaning "to strike with lightning." This makes sense. After all, the victim of a vicious *fulmination* may feel stung, almost as though he has just been struck by lightning.

garrulous (GAR uh lus)

excessively, tiresomely talkative *(adjective)*

 GABBY, RUDE, LOUD + S

A *garrulous* person isn't merely talkative. The word *garrulous* implies that the speaker is also boring, prone to rambling in an unstructured, redundant manner.

laconic (luh KON ik)

using few words; not talkative *(adjective)*

 LACk sONICs

The ancient Greek term for the Spartans is *Lakonikos*. The Spartans were famously well-disciplined soldiers who spoke little, which explains how *laconic* came to mean "not talkative."

lament (luh MENT)

to express grief; to mourn; to regret *(verb)*

 LAME END

Lamentations is a book in the Bible. It includes a series of poems *lamenting* the destruction of ancient Jerusalem.

pejorative (puh JAR uh tiv)

describing words and phrases intended to belittle others *(adjective)*

PrEJudiced ORATory + IVE

The word *pejorative* derives from the Latin word *peior*, which means "worse." So too does the word *impair* (meaning "to make worse through a reduction of strength or value").

rapport (ra POR)

a relationship of mutual trust and affinity (noun)

  RAPPer AND HIS COHORTs

The word *rapport* derives from the French word meaning "agreement." Often, two people who have a good *rapport* find themselves in agreement on a wide range of issues.

repartee (rep ur TAY)

a swift and witty reply; a conversation characterized by swift and witty replies *(noun)*

REPLIES ARE TOO CLEVER!

As you might have guessed from its spelling, *repartee* is French in origin. The French word *repartir* means "to retort" or "to respond wittily."

Unspoken

tacit (TASS it)

implied but not expressed; unspoken *(adjective)*

 TACk IT SHUT

The word *tacit* derives from the Latin word meaning "silent." It shares this root with the word *taciturn* (used to describe one whom prefers not to speak).

trite (TRYT)

unoriginal; overused; stale (*adjective*)

 TRIvial and TEdious

The word *trite* is often used to describe ideas that were once profound but which have become cliché through overuse.

wry (RY)

dryly humorous, often with a touch of irony *(adjective)*

 WITTY AND DRY

The word *wry* derives from the Middle English word meaning "to twist" or "to turn," probably because a *wry* comment is often twisted in meaning and usually accompanied by a twisted grin.

DRILLS

CHAPTER 3

I. Find the synonyms among the answer choices.

1. Which pair of words most nearly mean the same thing?
   a. biased - didactic
   b. adamant - emphatic
   c. rancorous - timorous
   d. frenetic - tepid

2. Which pair of words most nearly mean the same thing?
   a. candor - frankness
   b. enmity - camaraderie
   c. reticence - garrulity
   d. incorrigibility - stoicism

3. Which pair of words most nearly mean the same thing?
   a. lament - misquote
   b. laud - defile
   c. disparage - degrade
   d. parody - substantiate

4. Which pair of words most nearly mean the same thing?
   a. clandestine - amenable
   b. facetious - comical
   c. laconic - insolent
   d. intrepid - sonorous

5. Which pair of words most nearly mean the same thing?
   a. obscure - revere
   b. curtail - pervade
   c. abhor - mollify
   d. cavil - quibble

6.   Which pair of words most nearly mean the same thing?

   a. disparage - listless
   b. repartee - wry
   c. compelling – camaraderie
   d. emphatic- wary

II. Find the antonyms among the answer choices.

7.   Which pair of words are most nearly opposites?

   a. incorrigible - egregious
   b. feral - wild
   c. insolent - irascible
   d. reticent - garrulous

8.   Which pair of words are most nearly opposites?

   a. suppressed - unknown
   b. sanguine - lamenting
   c. decorous - proper
   d. wary - timorous

9.   Which pair of words are most nearly opposites?

   a. fulminate - laud
   b. glower - disguise
   c. vindicate - praise
   d. slander - denounce

10. Which pair of words are most nearly opposites?

   a. malicious - disingenuous
   b. cordial – brusque
   c. mercurial - temperamental
   d. conscientious - diligent

11. Which pair of words are most nearly opposites?
    a. exemplary - beatific
    b. affable - friendly
    c. egregious - obvious
    d. compelling - implausible

12. Which pair of words are most nearly opposites?
    a. tacit - spoken
    b. laudatory - praiseworthy
    c. discreet - secretive
    d. adamant - frenetic

III. Match the word in the left-hand column with the word or phrase in the right-hand column that is most similar in meaning.

13. laconic   a. instructive
14. didactic   b. clear
15. adage   c. belittling
16. rancorous   d. full of resentment
17. incisive   e. not talkative
18. trite   f. unoriginal
19. rapport   g. a wise saying
20. perjorative   h. a harmonious relationship

IF YOU CAN'T SAY ANYTHING NICE:

Words Describing Negative Attributes or Actions

biased (BY uhst)

prejudiced (adjective)

 BIGOTED HAYSEED

The word *bias* often refers to personal bigotry, as depicted by the misguided man above. It can also refer to a sampling error that skews poll results. This error is known as a *statistical bias*.

cantankerous (kan TANG kuhr us)

grumpy; disagreeable *(adjective)*

GET OUTTA HERE, YOU DARNED HOOLIGANS!

RANT HIS ANGER AT US

For some reason the word *cantankerous* has come to be associated almost exclusively with grumpy old people. We call grumpy young people quick-tempered and petulant; older grouches are also called crotchety and crusty.

caustic (KAW stik)

biting and sarcastic *(adjective)*

CAUSe hysTerICs

The word *caustic* can be used either as an adjective or as a noun. In its adjectival form, it describes something that burns, such as an acid or a scathing comment. As a noun, it describes a substance that can be used to burn, such as lye.

contumacious (kon too MAY shus)

disobedient, rebellious (adjective)

YOU CAN'T MAKE US!

The word *contumacious* has two noun forms with slightly different meanings. *Contumacy* means "headstrong rebelliousness"; *contumely* means "arrogant rudeness."

dilatory (DIL uh tor ee)

frequently late; extremely slow at work, causing delays *(adjective)*

THE LATE TORY

Another mnemonic device: *dilatory* sounds like delay. A *dilatory* person causes delays. (Note: Tories supported the British during the American Revolution.)

disdain (dis DAYN)

contempt, disrespect *(noun)*

  DISSING AND DARING

The word *disdain* describes a particular type of hatred, one fueled by complete contempt. In its verb form, to *disdain* someone or something is to treat it as unworthy of even the slightest respect.

duplicitous (doo PLIS i tus)

habitually deceptive; lying *(adjective)*

DUPE US

The word *duplicitous*, like *duplicate*, derives from the Latin word meaning "double." A less common meaning of *duplicitous* is "two-fold" or "doubled over."

fastidious (fuh STID ee us)

possessing careful attention to detail; difficult to please (adjective)

FUSSY, TIDY, TEDIOUS

The word *fastidious* often has a negative connotation, implying that the person being described is too attentive to details.

fractious (FRAK shus)

quarrelsome; unruly; likely to cause trouble *(adjective)*

FRACAS

A long time ago, the word *fraction* was commonly used to describe a state of disagreement between people. The word *fractious* takes its meaning from this obsolete usage of *fraction*. A *fractious* person is one who causes many disagreements.

glower (GLOU uhr)

to look or stare angrily or sullenly *(verb)*

 GEE! LOWER YOUR BROW!

The words *frown*, *glower*, and *scowl* all mean "to purse or contract eyebrows, indicating displeasure." *Frown* and *scowl* are synonyms. *Glower* is slightly different because it indicates that the frowner is staring at the source of his unhappiness.

haughty (HAW tee)

scornfully and condescendingly proud *(adjective)*

HIGH AND MIGHTY

The word *haughty* derives from the same root as the French word *haut*, meaning "high." Someone who is *haughty* looks down on everyone, as if from on high.

imperious (im PEER ee us)

arrogantly domineering, overbearing *(adjective)*

 IMPERIAL LOUSE

The words *imperious* and *empire* derive from the same Latin word meaning "to command." The word *imperious* implies that the person being described is too demanding.

indolent (IN duh lunt)

habitually lazy or inactive *(adjective)*

 IDLE

In England, they use the term "on the dole" to describe someone who receives government welfare payments. One who feels uncharitable toward the unemployed, might use "on the dole" as a mnemonic for *indolent*.

ingrate (IN grayt)

an ungrateful person *(noun)*

 AIN'T GRATEful

The words *grateful* and *gratitude* share the same Latin root with *ingrate*. The prefix in- means "not," so an *ingrate* is someone who is "not grateful."

insipid (in SIP id)

uninteresting; unchallenging; dull and tasteless *(adjective)*

IN YOU SIP, THEN SPIT

The word *insipid* combines the prefix in- (meaning "not") and the Latin word meaning "pleasing to the taste buds."

insolent (IN suh lunt)

insulting in manner or speech *(adjective)*

INSULTING GENT

The noun form of *insolent* is *insolence*. In old swashbuckler movies, someone invariably tells his enemy, "You shall pay for your *insolence*!" just before a sword fight begins.

irascible (ih RAS ih bul)

easily angered *(adjective)*

  IRATE AND UNSOCIABLE

The words *irascible*, *irate*, and *ire* all stem from the Latin word meaning "anger."

malevolent (muh LEV uh lent)

having or exhibiting ill will; wishing harm to others; malicious *(adjective)*

MATT IS ALWAYS VIOLENT

The word *malevolent* combines the Latin word *malus*, meaning "bad," and *volens*, meaning "to wish." Its literal meaning is "to wish ill of something or someone." The root *malus* also appears in *malice*.

malice (MA lis)

extreme ill will or spite *(noun)*

  MAD ALICE MAKES LICE

Many words that start with mal- have negative connotations. That's because they derive from the Latin word *malus*, which means "bad." *Malevolent* and *malady* are among the words that share this root with *malice*.

obdurate (OB duhr it)

stubborn *(adjective)*

OBSTINATE FOR THE DURATION

The Latin word *durus* means "hard." Other words sharing this root include *endure* (to withstand a difficult time by standing firm), *dour* (silent, gloomy, obstinate) and *duress* (forcible coercion, either through intimidation or actual violence).

obstinate (OB stuh nit)

stubborn, especially in holding an attitude, opinion, or course of action *(adjective)*

  OBSTRucTINg THE gATE

The Latin prefix ob- means "against." When added to the Latin word for "to stand" (*stinare*), it creates *obstinare*, meaning "to stand against." The word *obstinare* is the Latin predecessor of the English word *obstinate*.

parsimonious (pahr suh MO nee us)

excessively cheap (adjective)

PAUPER'S IN THE MONEY

The word *parsimonious* is used to indicate that a person or institution isn't merely frugal, but rather is cheap to a harmful extreme. A *parsimonious* businessman might refuse to invest in business improvements that would ultimately save him money because he can't stand to part with money, no matter how wisely it is spent.

repugnant (ri PUG nunt)

causing disgust or hatred; repulsive *(adjective)*

REPULSIVE PUG

The word *repugnant* derives from the Latin word meaning "to fight against." Because we fight against those things we find hateful, *repugnant* has come to mean "detestable."

unpalatable (un PAL uh tuh bul)

not pleasant; unpleasing *(adjective)*

UN+PAL-ABLE

The word *palate* refers to our sense of taste. Something that is *unpalatable*, then, is something that is unpleasing to our taste buds. The word *unpalatable* does not refer merely to bad food, however, but can be used to describe all unpleasant experiences.

DRILLS

CHAPTER 4

I. Match the word in the left-hand column with the word or phrase in the right-hand column that is most similar in meaning.

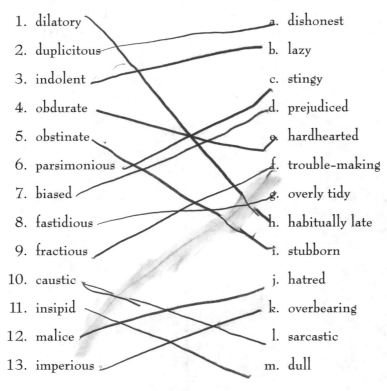

1. dilatory
2. duplicitous
3. indolent
4. obdurate
5. obstinate
6. parsimonious
7. biased
8. fastidious
9. fractious
10. caustic
11. insipid
12. malice
13. imperious

a. dishonest
b. lazy
c. stingy
d. prejudiced
e. hardhearted
f. trouble-making
g. overly tidy
h. habitually late
i. stubborn
j. hatred
k. overbearing
l. sarcastic
m. dull

II. Find the synonyms among the answer choices.

14. Which pair of words most nearly mean the same thing?
   a. cantankerous - irascible
   b. compelling - pejorative
   c. listless - frenetic
   d. diligent - ecstatic

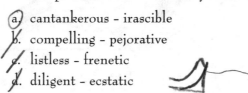

15. Which pair of words most nearly mean the same thing?
    a. staid – eclectic
    b. facetious – frank
    c. haughty – insolent
    d. malevolent – benevolent

16. Which pair of words most nearly mean the same thing?
    a. amenable – mercurial
    b. obstinate – contumacious
    c. furtive – egregious
    d. garrulous – implacable

17. Which pair of words most nearly mean the same thing?
    a. repugnant –unpalatable
    b. stoic – cordial
    c. tepid – torrid
    d. adamant – duplicitous

III. Find the opposite.

18. Which answer choice is the opposite of DISDAIN?
    a. mitigate
    b. respect
    c. exculpate
    d. fulminate

19. Which answer choice is the opposite of GLOWER?
    a. smile
    b. improve
    c. function
    d. stratify

20. Which answer choice is the opposite of MALEVOLENT?

  a. famished
  b. selfish
  c. charitable
  d. despicable

21. Which answer choice is the opposite of INGRATE?

  a. appreciative person
  b. overly active person
  c. person who is not famous
  d. sneaky person

THEM'S FIGHTING WORDS:
Words Relating to War and Combat

annihilate (uh NY uh layt)

to destroy completely *(verb)*

ANT HILL I ATE

The word *annihilate* contains the Latin word *nihil*, which means "nothing." As you can see, the aardvark above has just about *annihilated* the ant colony. A *nihilist* is someone who believes in nothing.

clandestine (klan DES tin)

secretive, usually with regard to concealing an illegal or unethical action *(adjective)*

CLOAK AND DAGGER

The word *clandestine* is most often applied to the actions of spies. *Clandestine* CIA operations uncovered by the American press include efforts to embarrass Fidel Castro and the assassination of Chilean president Salvador Allende.

conflagration (kon fluh GRAY shun)

a widespread fire *(noun)*

 CONTROVERSIAL FLAG ACTION

Extreme political upheaval, such as a riot, is sometimes referred to as a *conflagration*.

enmity (EN mi tee)

deep hatred, often mutually felt by two or more people or groups *(noun)*

  ENemy MIghTY angry

The words *enmity* and *enemy* share a Latin root. The word *enmity* is most often used to describe the specific type of hatred one feels for an *enemy*.

feral (FIR uhl)

savage, fierce, untamed; like a wild animal *(adjective)*

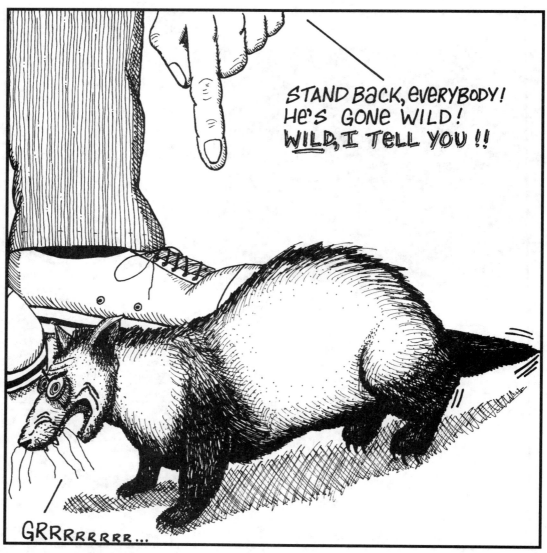

  FERRET WILL SCARE ALL

The word *feral* comes from the Latin word meaning "wild." The word *fierce* shares the same Latin root.

furtive (FUR tiv)

sneaky, stealthy *(adjective)*

 FUR-GɪTIVE

The word *furtive* is derived from the Latin word for "theft." This makes sense, since a thief has to be very sneaky to avoid getting caught! The fur-stealing fugitive pictured above is *furtively* getting away with his crime.

impede (im PEED)

to slow the progress of *(verb)*

LIMP KNEED

The noun form of *impede* is *impediment*. An *impediment* is something that slows progress, like a roadblock. In the illustration above, the man is clearly *impeded* by his limp knees.

intrepid (in TREP id)

courageous; fearless *(adjective)*

 INTRIGUED BY PITFALLS

The word *intrepid* combines the prefix in- (meaning "not") and the Latin word for "anxious" or "fearful." *Intrepid* is also the name of a veteran World War II aircraft carrier. Located in New York City, *Intrepid* is now a museum for World War II memorabilia and twentieth-century technology.

pacify (PA si fye)

to calm someone down; to soothe *(verb)*

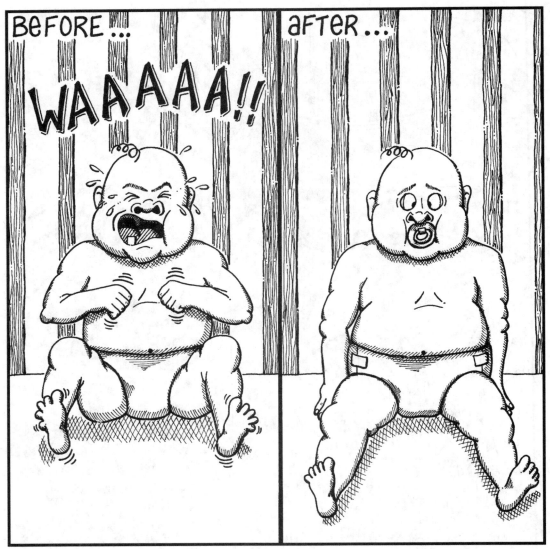

 PeACe-IFY

The word *pacify* stems from the Latin word *pax*, meaning "peace." Other words sharing this root include *pacific* (meaning "peaceful"), *appease* ("to calm"), and *peace*.

pugnacious (pug NAY shus)

combative; eager and enthusiastic to fight *(adjective)*

  A PUG NAMED viCIOUS

The word *pugnacious* derives from the Latin word for "fist." A pugnacious individual is one who is quick to use his fists.

ruse (ROOZ)

a crafty, often underhanded trick *(noun)*

 RULES ABUSED

The word *ruse* has a military origin and derives from the French word meaning "to drive back." Armies sometimes use *ruses* to "drive back" their enemies. The football player pictured above is creating a *ruse* to gain an unfair advantage.

stratagem (STRAT uh jum)

a clever trick used to deceive or outwit *(noun)*

  SET A TRAp ThAt GEts theM

The word *stratagem* derives from the ancient Greek word for "general," as in an army general. The general was, of course, the person responsible for coming up with *stratagems* to defeat the enemy.

surreptitious (sir rep TISH us)

done by secretive means *(adjective)*

 SURPRISED BY A REPTILE (+TIOUS)

The word *surreptitious* combines the prefix sub- (meaning "secretly") and the Latin word *rapere*, meaning "to seize." Other words sharing the same root include *rape*, *rapid*, and *ravish*.

thwart (THWART)

to prevent the occurrence of *(verb)*

THE WART

The wart on the nose of the poor guy above is clearly *thwarting* his chances of getting a date! There is also a lesser-known meaning of *thwart*; in its noun form, *thwart* refers to the seat in a rowboat on which the rower may sit.

timorous (TIM ur us)

shy; timid; fearful *(adjective)*

TIMID IN THE CHORUS

The word *timorous* comes from the Latin word meaning "to fear." The word *timid* shares the same root.

vilify (VIL uh fy)

to make vicious statements about *(verb)*

 VILLAIN-IFY

The word *vilify* comes from the Latin word meaning "worthless." *Vile* is another word with the same root.

wily (WY lee)

cunning *(adjective)*

 WIll B sLY

The coyote in *Road Runner* cartoons is named Wile E. Coyote. His name is an ironic pun, because he really isn't *wily* at all. A *wily* coyote would either figure out a way to catch a road runner, or go find something easier to catch!

DRILLS

CHAPTER 5

I. Match the word in the left-hand column with the word or phrase in the right-hand column that is most similar in meaning.

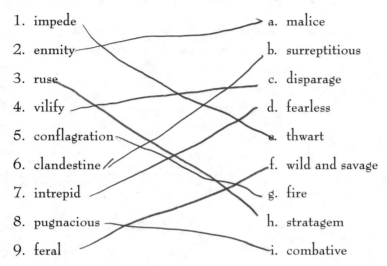

1. impede   a. malice

2. enmity   b. surreptitious

3. ruse   c. disparage

4. vilify   d. fearless

5. conflagration   e. thwart

6. clandestine   f. wild and savage

7. intrepid   g. fire

8. pugnacious   h. stratagem

9. feral   i. combative

II. Choose the word that best completes the meaning of the sentence.

10. Under cover of night, the army launched its _____ attack, hoping to catch the enemy by surprise.

    a. pejorative

    b. furtive

    c. timorous

    d. conscientious

11. Some psychiatrists believe that contact sports make participants more _____ and hostile in their everyday lives.

    a. reticent

    b. benevolent

    c. pugnacious

    d. compelling

12. The _____ soldier escaped the enemy camp by creating a ruse to dis-

tract the guards.

   a. frank
   b. clandestine
   (c.) wily
   d. dilatory

13. At the battle of Little Bighorn, the Sioux and Cheyenne _____ General George Custer's troops; no U.S. solder survived the battle.

   (a.) annihilated
   b. vilified
   c. pacified
   d. fulminated

14. The infantrymen advanced on the sergeant's order, all except for one _____ soldier who cowered in his trench, too frightened to join the fighting.

   a. intrepid
   b. parsimonious
   (c.) timorous
   d. furtive

15. The _____ refused to register for the military draft because he opposed all violence on principle.

   a. pugilist
   b. partisan
   (c.) pacifist
   d. pragmatist

LEGALESE:

Words Relating to Law and Order

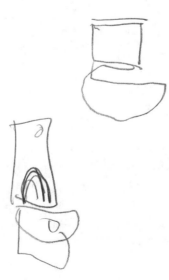

arbiter (AR bi tur)

a person who decides disputed issues *(noun)*

 ARGUMENT BISECTOR

The illustration above depicts the biblical king Solomon, who was asked to *arbitrate* a dispute between two women. Each claimed to be the mother of the disputed child. Solomon shrewdly suggested cutting the child in two. Solomon knew that the woman who was horrified by his suggestion was the true mother.

disingenuous (dis in JEN yoo us)

not straightforward; lacking in sincerity; pretending to know less than one actually does *(adjective)*

DIS AIN'T A GENUINE RESPONSE

The Latin word for "honest" is *ingenuus*. Add dis- and you get "not honest," the meaning of *disingenuous*.

egregious (ih GREE jus)

outrageously bad; clearly wrong or illegal *(adjective)*

🖐 EGG REGIS

The word *egregious* derives from the Latin prefix e- (meaning "apart from") and the noun *grex* (meaning "herd," "flock," or "crowd"). Something *egregious* is so obvious that, metaphorically speaking, it "stands apart from the crowd."

exculpate (EK skul payt)

to free from guilt or blame *(verb)*

 EX-CULPRIT

The Latin word for guilt is *culpa*. Besides *exculpate*, other words that incorporate this root include *culpable* and *culprit*.

fabricate (FAB ri kayt)

(1) concoct in order to deceive; (2) to create or build *(verb)*

 FABRIC dATE

A lie is sometimes euphemistically referred to as a *fabrication*. The two words mean the same thing, but for some reason *fabrication* doesn't sound as bad to most people.

heinous (HAY nus)

hatefully evil *(adjective)*

  HE Is NOt jUSt

The word *heinous* is related to the French word for hatred, *haine*. A *heinous* person is certainly worthy of hatred.

incorrigible (in KOR ih juh bul)

unable to be reformed; difficult to control *(adjective)*

ENCOURAGED TO BE HORRIBLE

The word *incorrigible* is often used to describe multiple-offense criminals, perhaps as "*incorrigible* recidivists." Badly behaved children frequently earn the label *incorrigible*.

jurisprudence (joor is PROOD uhns)

the philosophy or science of law; a system of laws *(noun)*

 JUstice RISes uP FROM RUles AND eviDENCE

The word *jurisprudence* combines the Latin words for "law" (*iuris*) and "knowledge" (*prudens*). The word means, literally, "knowledge of the law."

libel (LYE buhl)

a written or published falsehood injuring the reputation of the written piece's subject *(noun)*;
to lie maliciously in print about someone *(verb)*

LIE IN A TABLOID

There are many words in the English language to describe the various methods of spreading lies about another person. Aspersions are the subtlest, since they are statements that imply, but do not directly state, malicious insinuations. Slander and calumniate refer specifically to lies that are spoken. *Libel* refers to lies that appear in print.

litigious (lih TIJ us)

prone to filing lawsuits *(adjective)*

 LITTLE INJURIES, ENORMOUS LAWSUITS

The literal meaning of *litigious* is "relating to lawsuits." The word could, therefore, be used to describe all lawsuits, but its most common usage is to describe lawyers who file unnecessary or frivolous lawsuits.

notorious (no TOR ee us)

widely and unfavorably known; infamous *(adjective)*

 NOT GLORIOUS

The word *notorious* was once applied to both the famous and infamous, but its current usage favors the latter meaning almost exclusively, e.g., "the *notorious* gangster," "that *notorious* liar."

plausible (PLAW zi bul)

credible; appearing to be true *(adjective)*

PLENTY POSSIBLE

The word *plausible* shares its Latin root with *applause*, perhaps because a practical plan or a believable explanation is one that is worthy of praise.

slander (SLAN dur)

false charges and malicious statements about someone *(noun)*
to make false charges against someone *(verb)*

SLING DIRT

Lying about someone, especially if the lie is meant to cause harm, can be a crime. If the lie is spoken, the crime is *slander*. If the lie is printed (in a newspaper, for example), the crime is libel.

unfetter (un FEHT uhr)

set free of restrictions or bonds *(verb)*

RUN BETTER

A *fetter* is "a chain or shackle attached to the ankle or feet." *Fetters* have been used to restrict prisoners and slaves. To *unfetter*, then, literally means "to remove one's chains."

vindicate (VIN di kayt)

free from blame *(verb)*

 WIN THE CASE

Although its connotation today is generally positive, the word *vindicate* derives from the Latin word meaning "to avenge." It shares its origin with the word *vindictive*, which means "seeking revenge."

DRILLS

CHAPTER 6

I. Choose the best answer.

1. Which of the following words does NOT mean "to lie?"
   a. abhor
   b. fabricate
   c. slander
   d. libel

2. Which of the following words does NOT mean "to find innocent?"
   a. vindicate
   b. acquit
   c. cavil
   d. exculpate

3. Which of the following words would LEAST likely be used in a description of a vicious criminal?
   a. heinous
   b. incorrigible
   c. timorous
   d. notorious

II. Match the word in the left-hand column with the word or phrase in the right-hand column that is most similar in meaning.

4. arbiter C

5. disingenuous A

6. egregious G

7. jurisprudence F

8. litigious D

9. plausible B

10. unfettered E

a. dishonest

b. conceivable

c. referee

d. prone to filing lawsuits

e. free

f. the philosophy of law

g. obvious

HOW GOOD IS A POLITICIAN'S WORD?

Words Relating to Government

abdicate (AB duh kayt)

to formally give up power *(verb)*

ABANDON THE DICTATORSHIP

The word *abdicate* is most frequently used in reference to monarchs who renounce royal power. When they do so, we say that they have *abdicated* the throne.

cohesive (ko HEE siv)

sticking together *(adjective)*

 COHORT + adHESIVE TAPE

The word *cohesive* derives from the Latin word meaning "to cling." Other words sharing the same root are *adhesive* and *hesitate* (probably because someone who hesitates clings to a position instead of moving forward).

coup (KOO)

(1) a brilliantly executed plan; (2) a sudden overthrow of the government *(noun)*

 COok UPa PLAN

The word *coup* should not be confused with the word *coupe,* meaning "a two-door automobile."

despotic (de SPOT ik)

characterized by the exercise of absolute power, usually with evil intent *(adjective)*

 DESPicable pOliTICs

The word *despotic* derives from the Greek word meaning "master." Over the years, the word *despotic* came to refer specifically to overbearing, malicious rulers.

dictatorial (dik tuh TOR ee ul)

domineering; oppressively overbearing *(adjective)*

DICTATOR'S STYLE

The Latin word meaning "to speak" begins with the letters d-i-c. Other words sharing the same root are *Dictaphone* and *dictionary*.

dissident (DIS ih dint)

disagreeing with an established system, organization, or belief *(adjective)*

  DISSATISFIED stuDENT

The word *dissident* combines the prefix dis- (meaning "apart" or "away from") and the Latin word *sedere*, meaning "to sit." Literally, a *dissident* "sits apart" from the crowd.

impinge (im PINJ)

to encroach in a way that violates the rights of others; to trespass *(verb)*

 THE **IMP** INF**RINGE**s WHERE HE DOESN'T BELONG

The word *impinge* also means "to collide," as in the way sound waves *impinge* on the eardrum. However, the word *impinge* is typically used as a synonym for "trespass," as in the phrase "Please don't *impinge* on my personal space, Dad!"

itinerant (aye TIN uhr uhnt)

traveling from place to place *(adjective)*

ITINERARY MAN

The words *itinerant* and *itinerary* derive from the same Latin word meaning "road," "route," or "journey." An *itinerant* politician, for example, would use an *itinerary* to keep track of travel arrangements, scheduled meetings, and accommodations.

pander (PAN duhr)

to cater to the lower tastes and desires of others, or exploit their weaknesses *(verb)*

PANDA STANDER

The word *pander* is often used to describe the actions of politicians and always has a negative connotation. Liberals condemn huge tax cuts, and conservatives condemn new government spending programs, as *pandering* to the desires of their opponents. In the illustration above, the sideshow peddler is *pandering* to the circus crowd at the expense of the poor panda bear.

partisan (PAHR ti zun)

a devoted supporter *(noun)*; devoted to and biased toward a particular cause *(adjective)*

PARTY'S MAN

The word *partisan* is often seen and heard on the news in its adjectival form. News reports often refer to the *partisan* bickering or a *partisan* vote in Congress.

sanction (SANGK shun)

official permission or approval *(noun)*

 SANTA ACTIONS

Santa *sanctions*, or approves, the good behavior of little children by giving them gifts. A second meaning of *sanction* is "a penalty intended to encourage cooperative behavior." An example of this definition is the term *economic sanction*, such as the one the United Nations imposed on Iraq following the Gulf War.

suppress (suh PRESS)

to prevent from being known; to subdue *(verb)*

SUB + PRESS

The word *suppress* implies the use of considerable force. Freud aptly used the word *suppression* to describe the psychological mechanism by which the brain attempts to prevent unpleasant memories from surfacing. The man pictured above is *suppressing* information by pushing down on his briefcase, hence the root word "sub" (meaning below or secretly) in the mnemonic.

usurp (yoo SURP)

to take power by force *(verb)*

 USe yoUR Power

Some synonyms for *usurp* include arrogate, appropriate, and commandeer. Antonyms include surrender, yield, and relinquish.

DRILLS

CHAPTER 7

I. Choose the word (or words, when sentences have two blanks) to best complete the meaning of the sentence.

   1. The Bill of Rights guarantees that the government cannot _____ on the rights of individuals.

      a. pander

      b. impinge

      c. usurp

      d. glower

   2. Because the old king was too sick to rule, he _____ the throne to allow his son to take over the government.

      a. abdicated

      b. exculpated

      c. lauded

      d. distorted

   3. The president _____ the army's plan for a secret military strike by communicating his approval of it to the Joint Chiefs of Staff.

      a. alleviated

      b. curtailed

      c. usurped

      d. sanctioned

   4. President Richard Nixon filed suit to _____ the publication of the Pentagon Papers, but the Supreme Court ruled against Nixon and allowed American newspapers to reproduce the documents in their news stories.

      a. abet

      b. mollify

      c. suppress

      d. fabricate

5. Many Americans complain that the House of Representatives is too _____, with too many members rejecting negotiation and compromise, instead voting strictly along party lines.

   a. brittle
   b. partisan
   c. imperious
   d. itinerant

6. A diplomat leads a(n) _____ life, constantly traveling from one country to another.

   a. itinerant
   b. partisan
   c. benign
   d. heretical

7. The _____ group infiltrated the president's cabinet and led a _____ to overthrow the government.

   a. ornate – recitation
   b. dissident – coup
   c. innocuous – disparity
   d. tepid – plebiscite

8. The arrogant, _____ king did not seek honest advice from his counselors: rather, he sought out advisors who would _____ him and flatter him endlessly.

   a. cordial – critique
   b. eclectic – obscure
   c. pristine – disregard
   d. imperious – pander to

9. The CEO did not allow her subordinates much responsibility: rather, she was _____ in her insistence on supervising every aspect of the company.

   a. democratic
   b. dictatorial
   c. nonplused
   d. venal

10. American political parties are too large, and include too many people of differing opinions, to be very _____.
    a. cohesive
    b. dissident
    c. diffident
    d. nascent

11. The _____ dictator was feared by all of his subjects.
    a. cordial
    b. itinerant
    c. despotic
    d. partisan

EXTREME MEASURES:
Words Describing Degrees
of Importance

apropos (ap ruh PO)

opportune and relevant *(adjective)*

MAY YOU HAVE A LONG AND HAPPY MARRIAGE!

  APpROPriate wOrdS

The word *apropos* can also be used as a preposition meaning "concerning." One might say, for example, "*Apropos* your interest in building a better vocabulary, I would suggest The Princeton Review's excellent *Word Smart* series of books and tapes!"

defunct (di FUNGKT)

no longer effective or useful; having ceased to exist *(adjective)*

DE-FUNKED

The word *defunct* combines the prefix de- (to reduce, to undo, etc.) and the Latin word *fungi*, meaning "to perform." Literally, *defunct* means "having stopped performing."

degrade (di GRAYD)

to reduce in worth or value; to reduce in stature, rank, or grade *(verb)*

D GRADE

The word *degrade* combines the prefix de- (to reduce, to undo, etc.) with the Latin word *gradus*, meaning "step." Literally, the word means "to take down a step." Other words sharing this root include *gradation*, *centigrade*, and *graduate*.

eclectic (ih KLEK tik)

made up of a variety of sources or styles *(adjective)*

SELECT AND PICK

The word *eclectic* is often used to describe a person's tastes. It can also be used to describe an assortment—an eclectic mix of tropical fruits in a fruit basket, for example, might be made up of many fruits from different tropical regions all over the world.

gratuitous (gruh TOO ih tus)

given freely; unearned; unnecessary and unjustified *(adjective)*

 THIS TIP IS BETWEEN THE TWO OF US

The word *gratuitous* can have a positive connotation, as it does when it means "freely given" (e.g., "*gratuitous* charitable donation"). Remember, *gratuity* is another name for a tip you might leave at a restaurant. More often, however, the connotation is negative, meaning "uncalled for and unnecessary" (e.g. "*gratuitous* insult").

inconsequential (in kon suh KWEN shul)

unimportant (*adjective*)

MINOR CONSEQUENCES

The word *inconsequential* combines the prefix in- (meaning "not") and *consequential*, meaning "important."

incumbent (in KUM bint)

imposed as a duty; obligatory *(adjective)*

INCOME, BECAUSE OF THE RENT

As an adjective, *incumbent* means "obligatory," as in "It is *incumbent* on me to hand in my final paper by the deadline date." The word *incumbent* can also be a noun meaning "current office holder." When a president runs for reelection, for example, we refer to him as the *incumbent*.

prodigious (pro DIJ us)

enormous; impressively large; extraordinary *(adjective)*

PRODUCES BIG 'UNS

A person with *prodigious* talents—especially a very young person—is often referred to as a *prodigy*. The baseball player above has hit a *prodigious* home run.

superfluous (soo PER floo us)

extra; unnecessary *(adjective)*

SUPER FLUSH

The word *superfluous* derives from the Latin word meaning "to overflow." If the boy in the illustration above flushes one more time, the toilet might overflow!

tenuous (TEN yoo us)

uncertain; long and thin *(adjective)*

TENSE AND NERVOUS

The word *tenuous* derives from the Latin word *tenuis*, which means "thin." Other words with the same root include *attenuate* (which means "to stretch thin") and *extenuate* (which means "to lessen the severity of"; its original meaning was "to stretch thin").

DRILLS

CHAPTER 8

I. Match the word in the left-hand column with the word or phrase in the right-hand column that is most similar in meaning.

_g_	1. apropos	a.	uncertain
_d_	2. defunct	b.	obligatory
_c_	3. degraded	c.	reduced in value
_f_	4. inconsequential	d.	no longer useful
_b_	5. incumbent	e.	huge
_e_	6. prodigious	f.	unimportant
_a_	7. tenuous	g.	relevant

II. Find the synonyms among the answer choices.

8. Which pair of words most nearly mean the same thing?
   a. apropos – imperious
   b. dysfunctional – incumbent
   c. superfluous – gratuitous
   d. prophetic – inconsequential

III. Choose the word that best completes the meaning of the sentence.

9. Matty's _____ butterfly collection includes specimens from all over the world.
   a. convoluted
   b. eclectic
   c. heinous
   d. surreptitious

ANSWER KEY:
1. g   2. d   3. c   4. f   5. b
6. e   7. a   8. c   9. b

CHAPTER 9

DRAMATIC SPEECH:

Words Relating to the Arts

ad lib (ad LIB)

to improvise or deliver spontaneously *(verb)*

 ADds with LIBerty

The word *ad lib* is an abbreviation of the Latin term *ad libitum*, meaning "in accordance with one's wishes." A performer who *ad-libs* adds lines and gestures to a script in accordance with his or her wishes.

bombast (BAHM bast)

pompous, wordy speech or writing *(noun)*

 BOMB blAST OF WORDS

The word *bombast* derives from an older and obsolete English word, *bombace*, meaning "cotton padding." *Bombast* is the verbal equivalent of cotton padding: it adds bulk, but serves no other purpose.

embellish (em BELL ish)

to make beautiful by ornamenting; to add details, sometimes fictitious, to a story *(verb)*

EMBROIDER, WITH RELISH

The word *embellish* stems from the Latin word *bellus*, meaning "beautiful." Other words sharing this root include *belle* (a pretty woman), *beau* (a boyfriend), *beauty*, and *bibelot* (a small decorative object).

farce (FARS)

an absurdly ridiculous situation *(noun)*

FAR FETCHED

The word *farce* is frequently used to describe a type of movie, play, or novel. *Farces* have humorously exaggerated plots and characters. The Marx Brothers' *Duck Soup*, *A Day at the Races*, and *A Night at the Opera* are good examples of farces.

florid (FLOR id)

describing flowery or over-embellished speech *(adjective)*

![eye icon] **FLOWERY RIDdle**

The word *florid* derives from the Latin word for "flower." Other words sharing this root include *florist*, *floral*, and *flourish*.

hackneyed (HAK need)

overused and overly familiar; trivial *(adjective)*

 THAT HACK NEEDS SOME NEW IDEAS

A *hackneyed* idea or story is one that, at one time, was both fresh and interesting. Overuse, however, has turned that once-original idea into a trite cliché.

impromtu (im PROMP too)

spur of the moment; unplanned *(adjective)*

IMPulse PROMPTs yoU

The word *impromptu* often implies that an action is undertaken to address an unforeseen situation, e.g., an *impromptu* speech or *impromptu* emergency medical care.

lampoon (lam POON)

a broad piece of satire, usually ridiculing a person, group, or institution *(noun)*

CAMP TUNE

The National Lampoon is so called because it satirizes all aspects of American life and culture. The magazine grew out of the *Harvard Lampoon*, a humor magazine published by Harvard University students.

medley (MED lee)

an assortment or mixture, especially of songs or melodies *(noun)*

 MIX THE LETTERS OF MELODY TO (ALMOST) GET MEDLEY

Synonyms for *medley* include farrago, hodgepodge, gallimaufry, potpourri, and variety.

mural (MYOO rul)

a large painting applied directly to a wall or a ceiling *(noun)*

 PAINT YOUR WALL

Nearly all the world's cultures include *mural* painting among their arts. *Murals* over 10,000 years old have been discovered in French and Spanish caves. The most famous *murals* in the Western world are Michelangelo's wall and ceiling paintings at the Sistine Chapel in Rome.

parody (PAR o dee)

an artistic work that imitates the style of another, usually with comic intent *(noun)*

 PARrOt-y comeDY

Mad magazine is a magazine that parodies American culture for young audiences. *Saturday Night Live* also parodies a number of popular movies, television shows, and celebrities in its skits.

plagiarism (PLAY juh riz um)

to pass off another's ideas or writings as one's own *(verb)*

PLAYS I'VE WRITTEN

The word *plagiarism* derives from the Latin word meaning "to kidnap." In a figurative sense, a *plagiarist* "kidnaps" another person's ideas and claims them as his own.

poignant (POYN yunt)

emotionally moving; touching *(adjective)*

 POINT OF A ROMANTIC NOVEL

The word *poignant* derives from the Latin verb *pungere*, meaning "to pierce." Other words sharing the same root include *puncture*, *punctuate*, and *point*.

prosaic (pro ZAY ik)

unimaginative; dull *(adjective)*

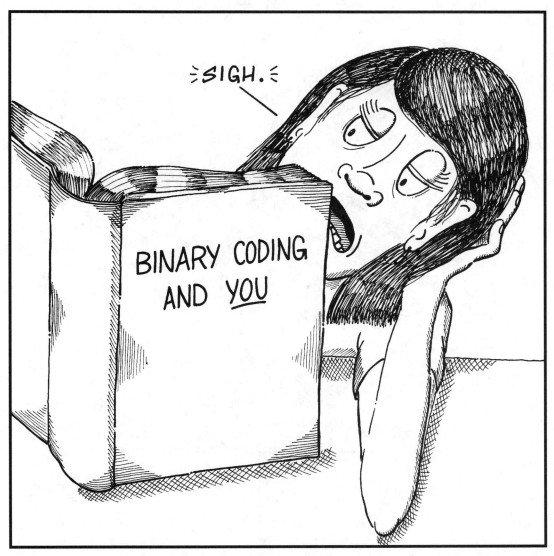

PROSE + ICK!

The words *prosaic* and *prose* share a common root. The word *prosaic* illuminates the distinction between poetry, which is imaginative and evocative, and prose, which conveys information in a useful but unexciting manner.

sonorous (SAHN uhr us)

having or producing sound *(adjective)*

 A SONG FOR US

The word *sonorous* simply means "sound-producing," but it is most often used to describe deep, rich sounds, such as those produced by acoustic guitars or bass singing voices.

terse (TURS)

brief and to the point; concise *(adjective)*

 TINY vERSE

American author Ernest Hemingway was famous for his *terse* writing. Many of the sentences in his novels are only a few words long.

DRILLS

I. Choose the best answer.

1. An actor who ad-libs does which of the following to the original script?
   a. She curtails it.
   b. She reveres it.
   c. She plagiarizes it.
   d. She embellishes it.

2. Which answer is most nearly the opposite of BOMBAST?
   a. florid
   b. terse
   c. brusque
   d. impromptu

3. A critic describes a novel as "hackneyed and prosaic." What does the critic mean?
   a. The novel is unoriginal and dull.
   b. The novel is plagiarized and full of grammatical errors.
   c. The novel is well written and exciting.
   d. The plot of the novel is implausible.

4. A painting executed on a wall is called a _____.
   a. lampoon
   b. farce
   c. mural
   d. parody

5. Which of the following is most likely to be used to describe great singing?
   a. trite
   b. sonorous
   c. caustic
   d. insolent

6. The singer performed a continuous piece of music that included one verse from each of his hit records. That piece of music could be referred to as a _____.

   a. mural
   b. medley
   c. conflagration
   d. plagiarism

7. Which of the following does NOT necessarily refer to a comic artwork?
   a. farce
   b. lampoon
   c. parody
   d. pantomime

II. **Match the word in the left-hand column with the word or phrase in the right-hand column that is most nearly its opposite.**

8. plagiarism	a. overly wordy
9. florid	b. short and to the point
10. impromptu	c. unmoving
11. poignant	d. original writing
12. terse	e. well-planned

THAT'S A LOT OF SCIENTIFIC MUMBO JUMBO:
Words Relating to the Sciences

aberration (ab uh RAY shun)

a deviation from the way things normally occur or are performed *(noun)*

 A VERY RARE VARIATION

The word *aberration* has several specific technical applications. In psychology, it refers to abnormal behavior; in astronomy, it refers to the illusion of displacement of a celestial body caused by the motion of the earth; and in genetics, it is used to describe abnormalities in chromosomal structure.

catalog (KAT uhl og)

to make an itemized list of *(verb)*

 CApTAin's LOG

The Dewey Decimal System is a way of cataloging library books. These numbers are recorded in a library's catalog, which most modern libraries have on computer.

debunk (dee BUNK)

to expose the falseness of; to disprove *(verb)*

DE (AS IN UN) + BUNK

To *debunk* something is to expose it as "bunk." The word *bunk* not only means "a type of bed," but it also means "nonsense." It is the latter meaning of *bunk* to which the word *debunk* refers. People rarely use this meaning of *bunk* anymore, but if you watch old movies you're likely to see a character say derisively, "Aw, that's a lot of *bunk*!"

disparate (DIS puh rit)

fundamentally distinct or different *(adjective)*

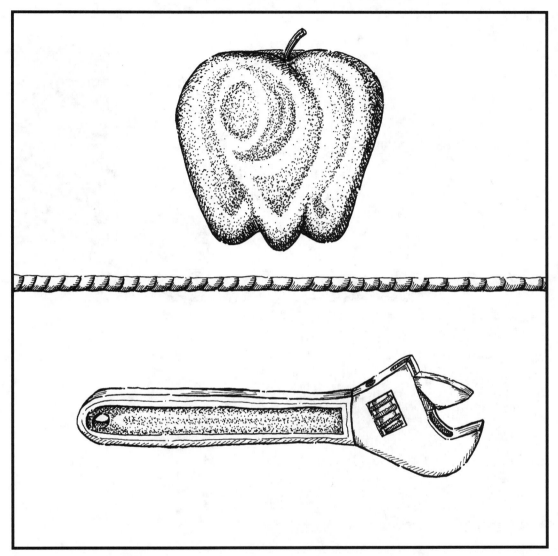

 ## DISTINCT AND SEPARATE

The noun form of *disparate* is *disparity*, which means "the state of being unequal." If two friends drew very different salaries, they might discuss the *disparity* in their incomes. Two things might be considered as *disparate* as an apple and a wrench.

dubious (DOO bee us)

doubtful, unlikely to be true or authentic *(adjective)*

 I DoUBt It, it's bOgUS

The words *dubious*, *indubitable*, and *doubt* all derive from the same Latin word meaning "doubt."

feasible (FEE zi bul)

possible *(adjective)*

  THE **FEAS**T IS POSS**IBLE**

The word *feasible* is a cousin to the French word *faire*, meaning "to do" or "to make." This makes sense. Something that is *feasible* is doable.

fluid (FLOO id)

easily flowing; elegant and graceful *(adjective)*

FLOW LIKE LIQUID

By considering the meaning of the noun *fluid*, it is easy to figure out how the adjective *fluid* got its meaning. Something that moves *fluidly* flows easily, like a liquid.

incontrovertible (in kon truh VUR tuh bul)

indisputable; not open to question *(adjective)*

 CONTROVERSIAL TO CONTRADICT

As you might have guessed, *incontrovertible* shares its Latin root with *controversy*. Something that is *incontrovertible* is *uncontroversial*; the prefix in- serves the same negating function as does the prefix un-.

innate (ih NAYT)

inborn; possessed at birth *(adjective)*

 INNer fATE

The word *innate* derives from the Latin word *nasci*, meaning "to be born." With the prefix in- added, it's easy to see how the word came to mean "inborn."

meticulous (mi TIK yuh luhs)

extremely careful and precise *(adjective)*

MEga-parTICULar (+ OUS)

The word *meticulous* is often used to describe someone who is extremely concerned with details, such as a scientist. Someone who has every hair in place, every pant crease ironed, and every inch of shoe perfectly polished is said to be *meticulously* groomed.

nascent (NAY suhnt)

having recently come into existence; emerging (adjective)

NEW SCENT

The Latin root of *nascent* is the word meaning "to be born." Other words sharing the same root include *natal*, *native*, *nature*, *innate*, and *renaissance*.

pragmatic (prag MA tik)

practical (adjective)

PRACTICAL, NOT ROMANTIC

The word *pragmatic* derives from the Latin word meaning "skilled in business." Over time, the word has come to mean "skilled" in all types of practical matters.

punctilious (punk TIL ee us)

strictly attentive to minute details; precise *(adjective)*

PUNCTUAL IS US

A *punctilio* is a "fine point of etiquette." One who is *punctilious* knows and conforms to society's many *punctilios*.

substantiated (sub STAN she ayt id)

supported with proof or evidence; verified *(adjective)*

 SUBSTANCE IS VALIDATED

Some synonyms for *substantiated* include validated, verified, authenticated, and corroborated. Antonyms include disproved, refuted, discredited, and undermined.

DRILLS

I. Choose the word or pair of words that best completes the meaning of the sentence.

1. None of the scientists found the theory _____ until confronted with _____ proof of its accuracy.
   a. fractious – trite
   b. pragmatic – irresponsible
   c. feasible – incontrovertible
   d. substantiated – suspect

2. In her examination of the patient's skin graft, the doctor noted that nearly all the cells were exactly the same; however, she also found some _____ in the sample.
   a. aberrations
   b. stratagems
   c. fabrications
   d. dissidents

3. Scientists from the American Cancer Society have many times _____ the contention of tobacco industry scientists that cigarettes cannot be linked to cancer.
   a. substantiated
   b. debunked
   c. vindicated
   d. parodied

4. A few skeptical researchers remained _____ of the study despite the fact that its data appeared to be well _____.
   a. dubious – substantiated
   b. farcical – fabricated
   c. unconvinced – debunked
   d. reticent – fulminated

5. Psychologists debate whether intelligence is _____ or whether it is acquired after birth through socialization.
    a. didactic
    b. innate
    c. caustic
    d. despotic

6. In its _____ stage, a chicken is an egg.
    a. nascent
    b. dormant
    c. waning
    d. hackneyed

7. The high school physics teacher said: "Let's be _____; as much as we may want one, we will probably never have a particle accelerator here at our school."
    a. idyllic
    b. tepid
    c. pragmatic
    d. ebullient

8. Carolus Linnaeus created the binomial system of nomenclature as a means of _____ plants and animals.
    a. debunking
    b. degrading
    c. pandering
    d. cataloging

II. Match the word in the left-hand column with the word or phrase in the right-hand column that is most similar in meaning.

9. disparate

10. fluid

11. meticulous

a. graceful

b. punctilious

c. dissimilar

SPEAKING PRECIPITOUSLY:
Words Relating to the Weather

arid (A rid)

dry, rainless; primarily used to describe climates *(adjective)*

  AREA RID OF WATER

Although usually used to describe climatic conditions, the word *arid* is occasionally used to describe an emotionless or dry work of literature or art, e.g., "an *arid* book lacking emotional impact."

idyllic (aye DIL ik)

simple, carefree; peaceful *(adjective)*

IDEAL-LIKE

In poetry, an *idyll* is a short poem that celebrates rural setting. *Idylls* typically describe soft green grass, warm sunny days, cool shade, the gentle grazing of peaceful animals, and the simple dignified lives of rural people. They are usually written by city dwellers.

ominous (AH mi nus)

menacing; threatening *(adjective)*

  BOMb IN THE HOUSe

People often use the word *ominous* to describe weather conditions. "*Ominous* clouds," for example, mean that rain is likely.

serene (suh REEN)

calm, peaceful (*adjective*)

SEA OF GREEN

The word *serene* is often used to describe peaceful weather conditions. A person with great peace of mind, such as a spiritual religious leader is described as *serene*.

temperate (TEM puhr it)

moderate; mild *(adjective)*

  TEMPERATurE IS GREAT

The word *temperate* has many uses. It can apply to the weather (a *temperate* climate), to a person's disposition (a *temperate* individual), or to a speech or book (a *temperate* analysis of the situation).

wane (WAYN)

to decrease gradually; to fade *(verb)*

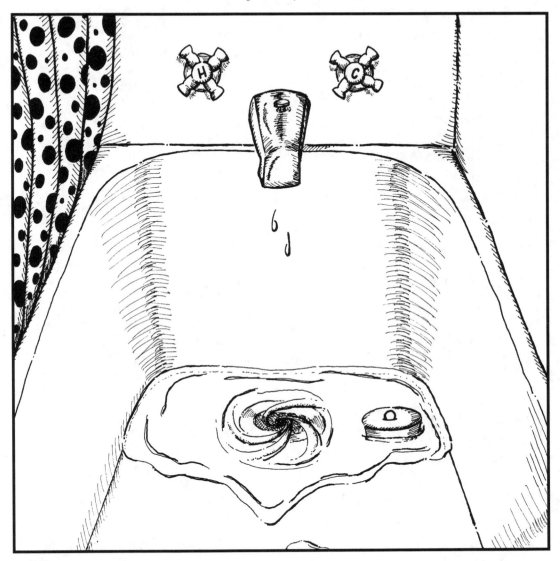

 THE WATERS WANE DOWN THE DRAIN

The word *wane* is used to describe the phases of the moon. During the first half of the lunar month—as the moon appears to increase in size—we say the moon is waxing. During the second half of the month—as the moon appears to decrease in size—we say the moon is *waning*.

DRILLS

CHAPTER 11

I. **Select the best answer.**

1. Which of the following is LEAST applicable to a beautiful, sunny, cloudless day?
    a. idyllic
    b. serene
    c. ominous
    d. temperate

2. Which of the following words is most likely to be used in a description of the desert?
    a. arid
    b. tropical
    c. humid
    d. arctic

3. During the two weeks following a full moon, the lit portion of the moon grows smaller with each passing night. Which word is used to describe this process?
    a. slander
    b. waning
    c. laud
    d. pander

ANSWER KEY:
1. c 2. a 3. b

TAKING THE HIPPOCRATIC OATH:
Words Relating to Medicine

alleviate (uh LEE vee ayt)

to ease a pain or burden *(verb)*

RELIEVE THE ACHE

The Latin root of *alleviate* is the adjective meaning "light." Other words sharing the same root include *levitate* (to cause to float) and *levity* (lightness of attitude, often bordering on frivolity).

benign (bi NYNE)

kind and gentle; harmless *(adjective)*

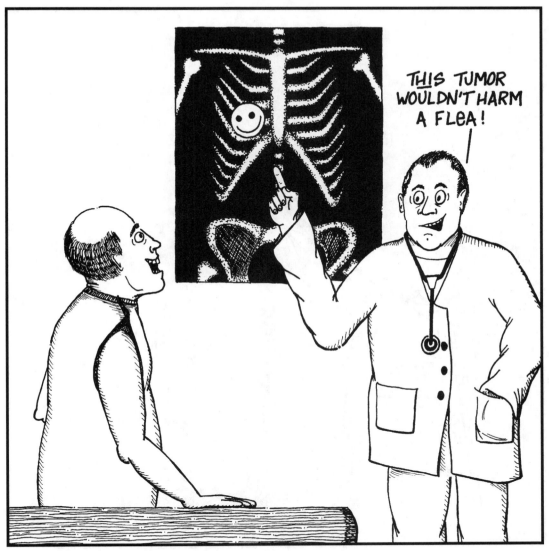

BE NICE

The word *benign* has become closely associated with the medical term *"benign* tumor," meaning "a tumor that causes no harm." The word *benign* can also be used to describe people and things that are beneficial—for example, "a *benign* personality," "a *benign* climate"—as well as those things that are non-harmful.

brittle (BRIT uhl)

easily broken when subjected to pressure *(adjective)*

 BRoken LITTLE old man

Peanut brittle is a type of peanut-and-toffee candy bar that breaks very easily. That's why it's called peanut brittle.

deleterious (deh li TEER ee us)

having a harmful effect; injurious *(adjective)*

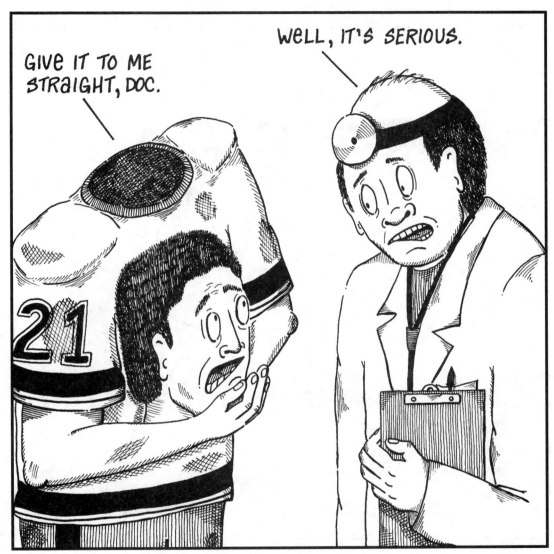

 WELL, IT'S SERIOUS

The word *deleterious* is often used to describe an unexpected harmful effect, e.g., "the deleterious effects of taking vitamin supplements."

emollient (ih MOLL yuhnt)

softening and soothing; making less harsh or abrasive *(adjective)*
a softening and soothing agent, such as a skin cream *(noun)*

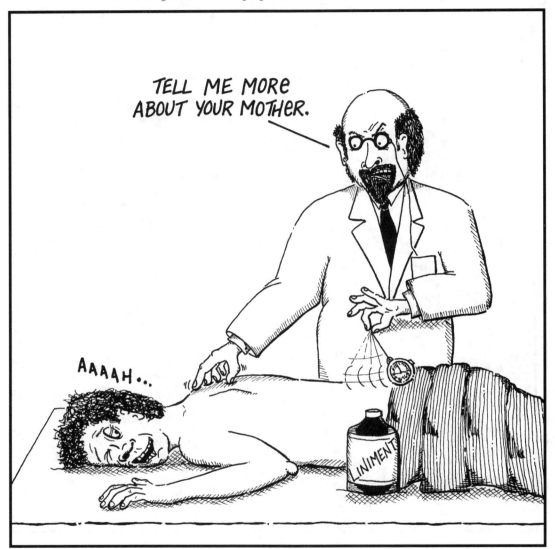

 EMOTionaL LInimENT

The Latin root of *emollient* is *mollis*, meaning "soft." The word *mollify* (an adjective meaning "to soothe or soften") shares the same root.

febrile (FEB ruhl)

relating to or characterized by fever *(adjective)*

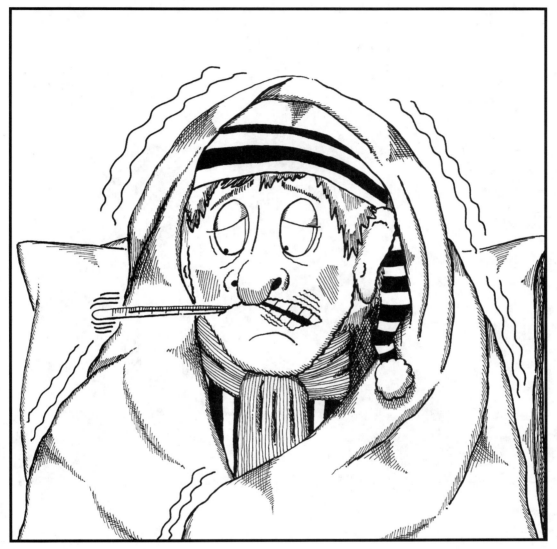

 FEver BuRns whILE you shiver

The Latin word for "fever" is *febris*. Other words that share this root include *fever* and *febrifacient* (meaning "something that causes a fever").

innocuous (ih NOK yoo us)

harmless (adjective)

UN-NOXIOUS

The Latin word *nocuus* means "harmful." Add the prefix in- and you have the meaning of *innocuous*, "not harmful." Have you ever been to the doctor for an *inoculation*? (We hope so!)

mollify (MOL uh fye)

to calm or soothe *(verb)*

MAKE OLLIE FINE

The Latin root of *mollify* is *mollis*, meaning "soft." The word *emollient* (an adjective meaning "making softer and smoother") shares the same root. (That's Oliver Hardy, the old-time comedian, in the picture.)

pristine (pris TEEN)

pure, unspoiled, immaculate *(adjective)*

IT'S CLEAN

The word *pristine* is often used to describe areas untouched by human visitors, as in *"pristine* wilderness."

soporific (sop uh RIF ik)

causing sleep or sleepiness *(adjective)*; a drug that causes sleep *(noun)*

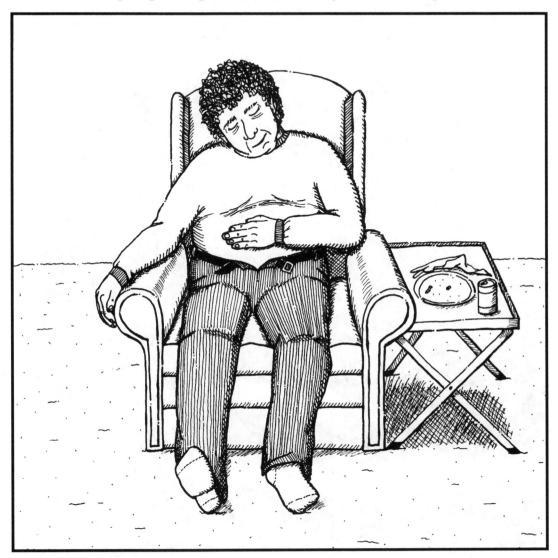

SUPPER WAS TERRIFIC

The suffix –fic means "making." *Sopor* is the Latin word for "sleep." Thus, *soporific* means "makes one sleep."

toxic (TOKS ik)

poisonous *(adjective)*

 IT MADE TODD SICK

The ancient roots of the word *toxic* reach back to the Greek word for "bow"—*toxon*—as in "bow and arrow." When the ancient Greeks developed a poison to apply to their arrows, they called it *toxikon*.

DRILLS

CHAPTER 12

I. Match the word in the left-hand column with the word or phrase in the right-hand column that is most similar in meaning.

1. benign
2. brittle
3. deleterious
4. febrile
5. emollient
6. pristine
7. soporific

a. sleep-inducing
b. harmless
c. immaculate
d. harmful
e. feverish
f. easily broken
g. softening

II. **Find the antonym.**

8. Which answer is most nearly the opposite of TOXIC?

   a. remote
   b. innocuous
   c. exemplary
   d. ebullient

9. Which answer is most nearly the opposite of MOLLIFY?

   a. irritate
   b. alleviate
   c. pander
   d. ad-lib

ANSWER KEY:
1. b 2. f 3. d 4. e 5. g
6. c 7. a 8. b 9. a

MONEY TALKS:
Words Relating to Money and Wealth

milk

to extract money or other benefits from *(verb)*

MILK MONEY

This meaning of *milk* represents the cynic's view of cows as nothing more than a source of income. The common phrase to "*milk* someone dry" further indicates the cynicism of this use of the word *milk*.

opulent (OP yoo lunt)

possessing or exhibiting abundant wealth *(adjective)*

TOP PERCENT OF EARNERS

The word *opulent* derives from the Latin word *opus*, meaning "work." The implication is clear. If you work hard, you may become extremely wealthy!

ornate (or NAYT)

elaborately decorated *(adjective)*

 ORNAMENTS BY THE CRATE

The root of *ornate* is the Latin word *ornāre*, meaning "to decorate or embellish." Other words with the same root include *ornament* and *adorn*.

ostentatious (ahs ten TAY shus)

showy, done to make an impression *(adjective)*

 COST IN YOUR FACE (+IOUS)

The noun form of *ostentatious* is *ostentation* (meaning "showiness"). The words *ostensible* and *ostensive* mean "apparent," as in "Joe's *ostensible* reason for going to the library was to study, but we think he really just wanted to flirt with girls."

paucity (PAW si tee)

extreme lack of; smallness of number *(noun)*

SAUCE PITY

As illustrated above, the *paucity* of sauce on the pasta is a pity! Another way to remember *paucity* is to see that it begins with the same three letters as the word *pauper*. A *pauper* is someone with a *paucity* of money and possessions.

solvent (SAHL vunt)

able to pay one's debts *(adjective)*

  SOLVes THE rENT PROBLEM

In chemistry, a *solvent* is a chemical that can dissolve another substance. Turpentine, for example, is a *solvent* for oil paints.

squalor (SKWAL uhr)

a filthy condition or quality *(noun)*

 SQUAsh + sLObbeR

The word *squalor* implies some type of illicit or sordid detail. People who live in *squalor* are not merely filthy, but rather are filthy because of their decrepitude e.g., "the *squalor* of the heroin addict's apartment."

urbane (ur BAYN)

notably polite and elegant; suave, sophisticated *(adjective)*

 URBAN-Y

The word *urbane* derives from the Latin word meaning "from the city." It reflects the belief that city people are polite and civilized, while country people are uncouth and uneducated.

DRILLS

CHAPTER 13

I. Select the best answer.

1. A real estate developer builds a new high-rise office complex. The extremely expensive building features pink marble walls, a man-made waterfall, generous amounts of chrome plating, and a gallery of exclusive, high-price boutiques and jewelry stores. A person would be LEAST likely to use which of the following words in describing this building?

    a. opulent
    b. ornate
    c. obstinate
    d. ostentatious

2. Which word best describes a business that can meet all its financial obligations?

    a. solvent
    b. stymied
    c. soporific
    d. squalid

3. A local opera company canceled a performance because only ten tickets were sold, and as a result the company did not have enough money to rent the theater. Which of the following states the reason that the performance was canceled?

    a. copious ticket sales
    b. a paucity of ticket revenues
    c. ample audience interest in the performance
    d. auspicious advance ticket purchases

4. The penny-pinching factory owner worked his employees to the bone while paying them next to nothing. Which of the following best describes what he is doing to his workers?

    a. he is milking them
    b. he is lauding them
    c. he is vindicating them
    d. he is revering them

5. Jennifer enjoys living in the city where she can take advantage of its many museums, art galleries, and film events. Which of the following would be used to best describe Jennifer?

a. opulent
b. urbane
c. idyllic
d. punctilious

SAY A LITTLE PRAYER:
Words Relating to Matters of Faith

austere (aw STEER)

somber; stern and severe *(adjective)*

 AUnt STERnEst

The word *austere* is often used to describe people who are not only stern, but also strict and unsympathetic. Puritans are often described as *austere*.

beatific (bee uh TIF ik)

revealing profound joy and inner peace; angelic *(adjective)*

  BEAming TerriFICally

The word *beatific* often has religious implications: saints, mystics, bodhisattvas, and other enlightened religious figures are frequently described as *beatific*. The Roman Catholic Church honors a select few after death through a process called *beatification*, which elevates the honoree to a status somewhere between mere mortality and sainthood.

cloister (KLOY stuhr)

a peaceful, secluded place; a place devoted to religious retreat, such as a monastery (noun)
to seclude, especially for the purpose of religious devotion and contemplation (verb)

CLOSED TO OUTSIDERS

The word *cloister* derives from the Latin word *claustrum*, meaning "an enclosed place." *Claustrophobia*, meaning "fear of enclosed places," shares the same root.

emulate (EM yuh layt)

to try to equal or excel, especially through imitation *(verb)*

 EMU I'lL imitATE

An emu is a tall, flightless bird resembling the ostrich. In the computer world, the word *emulate* is used to describe how one computer system can be taught to perform the functions of another. With the right software, for example, an Apple computer can *emulate* a PC; that is, it can run PC programs and read PC documents.

epiphany (ih PIF uh nee)

a sudden burst of understanding or discovery; a revelation, often of a religious nature *(noun)*

 EPISODE ISN'T PHONY

Epiphanies is a Christian feast holiday celebrating the Magi's discovery of the baby Jesus. The holiday symbolically commemorates the revelation of the divinity of Jesus to Christians.

harbinger (HAR bin juhr)

one that foreshadows or announces the arrival of an event or individual *(noun)*

 HARBor rINGer means dangER

Someone who constantly predicts negative results is referred to as a *harbinger* of doom.

heresy (HAIR ih see)

an opinion that differs from established, dearly held beliefs, often of a religious nature *(noun)*

HEATHENS REALLY SAY THESE THINGS

The adjectival form of *heresy* is *heretical*. Those who hold *heretical* beliefs are called *heretics*.

omnipotent (om NIP uh tuhnt)

possessing unlimited power (adjective)

I'M IMPORTANT

The word *omnipotent* combines the Latin prefix omni-, meaning "all," with the adjective *potens*, meaning "powerful." Gods are usually referred to as *omnipotent*.

penitent (PEN ih tunt)

expressing remorse or regret for one's misdeeds *(adjective)*

 PENITENTiary

A *penitent* in the Catholic Church is someone who seeks forgiveness for his sins. He is usually assigned *penance*, in the form of prayers or charitable actions, as the means of achieving forgiveness. In Judaism, the holiest day of the year is Yom Kippur, the Day of *Penitence*.

pious (PYE us)

devout; moral *(adjective)*

 PIcture Of jUStice

Although the word *pious* usually has a positive connotation, it has a less frequently used negative meaning. Sometimes *pious* is used to describe someone who wishes to come across as moral but who in fact is not, as in the statement "I hate that *pious*, self-righteous hypocrite!"

portend (por TEND)

to serve as an omen or warning of *(verb)*

 rePORT THE END

Something that *portends* an event is called a "portent" or an "omen." The adjective used to describe such things is *portentious*.

precept (PREE sept)

a principle establishing proper behavior *(noun)*

PREaching acCEPTed

A *precept* is often religious in nature, as is a tenet. A collection of related *precepts* is sometimes referred to as a canon or catechism.

prophetic (pruh FET ik)

foretelling or predicting future events *(adjective)*

 PROPHET-LIKE

Prophets figure prominently in ancient literature. Famous prophets include Cassandra, who was cursed to preach the truth to unbelieving audiences; Jonah, whose defiance landed him in God's doghouse (or whale-house, more accurately); and John the Baptist, who *prophesied* the coming of Jesus.

purist (PYOO rist)

one who is particularly concerned with maintaining traditional practices *(noun)*

 PURᴇ, ɪs ɪᴛ?

The word *purist* derives from the Latin word meaning "pure." Other words sharing the same root include: *purify*, *Puritan*, *purge* (meaning "to *purify* by expelling impurities"), and purée (meaning "to blend and strain food, thereby making it *pure*").

reclamation (re cluh MAY shun)

a restoration to productivity or usefulness *(noun)*

 RECLAIM A NATION

The word *reclamation* is the noun form of the verb *reclaim*. When a deposed ruler *reclaims* the throne, for example, that leader makes a *reclamation* of power.

revere (ruh VEER)

to greatly respect and honor *(verb)*

REVEal REspect

Many Protestant religious leaders are referred to as *reverend*, a word that shares its Latin root with the word *revere*. As a religious leader, a *reverend* should be *revered* by his or her congregation.

zealous (ZEHL us)

passionate; extremely interested in pursuing something *(adjective)*

ZESTY FELLAS

The word *zeal* is often used to describe a passion for a particular cause or area of interest, e.g., "a *zealous* environmentalist," "a *zealous* student of the classics." Fanatics, especially religious fanatics, are sometimes referred to as *zealots*.

DRILLS

CHAPTER 14

I. Match the word in the left-hand column with the word or phrase in the right-hand column that is most similar in meaning.

1. epiphany	a.	omen
2. harbinger	b.	unorthodox belief
3. heresy	c.	holy
4. reclamation	d.	capable of foreseeing the future
5. omnipotent	e.	predict
6. penitent	f.	adore
7. pious	g.	enlightening experience
8. portend	h.	seeking forgiveness
9. precept	i.	restoration to use
10. prophetic	j.	a rule
11. revere	k.	extremely passionate
12. zealous	l.	all-powerful

II. Choose the word or pair of words that best completes the meaning of each sentence.

13. The Puritan church was an _____ building with little ornamentation.
   a. austere
   b. opulent
   c. inveterate
   d. ad-libbed

14. "I want to be just like the saints," said Patrick; "I want to _____ their virtues."
   a. abjure
   b. stymie
   c. truncate
   d. emulate

15. Before her visit to the retreat, May was confused and frantic but when she returned she was rested, serene, and _____.

    a. zealous
    b. soporific
    c. beatific
    d. ostentatious

16. A critic wrote the following about a rock opera: "I don't like it. I don't believe in mixing two art forms; the result is invariably the corruption of both." Which of the following best describes the critic?

    a. a purist
    b. a dabbler
    c. a despot
    d. a caviler

17. When she wanted to be alone, Celine _____ herself in her room.

    a. cataloged
    b. cloistered
    c. convoluted
    d. caviled

DIMENSIONS:

Words Relating to Time and Space

ample (AM pul)

describing a large amount of something (adjective)

I AM PLEnty BIG

The Latin root of ample is amplus, meaning "large." This root can also be found in such words as amplifier (an amplifier makes things larger or louder) and amplitude (the amplitude of a thing is the measure of its how large it is).

archaic (ar KAY ik)

old-fashioned; outdated *(adjective)*

ARCHAeOLOGICAL RelIC

When something is described as *archaic*, the implication is that it is not only old, but is also primitive. Your great-grandfather is old; his rotary telephone is *archaic*.

behemoth (bi HEE muth)

something that is large, very powerful, or both *(noun)*

BIG, HEAVY MOTHER

The word *behemoth* derives from the Hebrew word meaning "beast." The word found its way into the English language via the Bible.

burgeon (BUR juhn)

expand or grow rapidly *(verb)*

BURGErs, ONe after another

For centuries, the word *burgeon* was used only to describe plants. The word meant "to put forth buds or leaves." In the last forty years, however, its usage has expanded—or *burgeoned*!—to its more general meaning of "to grow rapidly." Today, anything that grows rapidly can be said to *burgeon*.

capacious (kuh PAY shus)

roomy, spacious *(adjective)*

  THE CAP IS TOO SPACIOUS

The word *capacious* shares its Latin root with the word *capacity*, which is the maximum amount or number that can be enclosed in a certain space. The *capacity* of an arena, for example, is the maximum number of people that the arena can seat.

copious (KO pee us)

plentiful; large in quantity *(adjective)*

 COPIer gOes nUtS

The Latin root of *copious* is *copia*, meaning "abundance." The root is also found in the English word *cornucopia* (literally "a horn of plenty," *cornucopia* also means "a great abundance," e.g., "television, a *cornucopia* of entertainment").

curtail (kur TAYL)

to cut short; abbreviate *(verb)*

 THE MOUSE HAS A CURT tAIL

Etymologists believe that the words *curtail* and *tailor* (whose job, after all, is to cut cloth), are derived from the same Middle English word meaning "to cut."

inveterate (in VET ur it)

deep-rooted; set in one's ways *(adjective)*

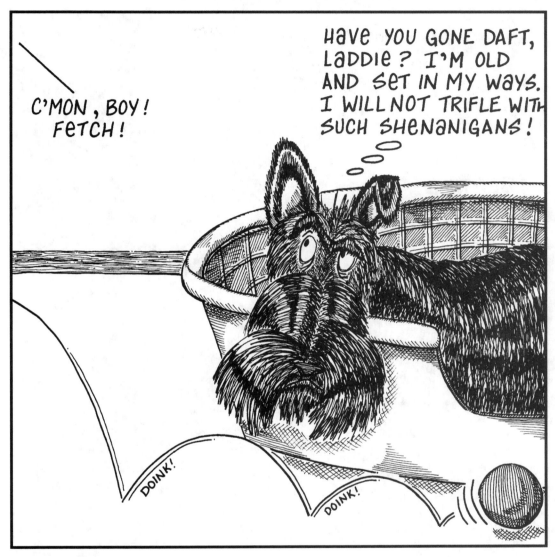

INVariable, ETERnAl TErrier

The root of *inveterate* is the Latin word meaning "old." The word *veteran* (a person with great experience) shares the same root.

nocturnal (nok TUR nuhl)

active at night; occurring at night *(adjective)*

CLOCK SPURNER AL

In many languages, the word for "night" incorporates some variant of noct-. In German, the word is *nacht*; in Spanish, *noches*. The French *nuit* is a close cousin to *nacht*, *noches*, and *nocturnal*.

novel (NAH vuhl)

strikingly new, unusual, or different *(adjective)*

 NOVELty STORE

The word *novel* implies that the thing being described isn't merely new but is also original and unusual. One might say this book presents a *novel* approach to vocabulary building.

permeate (PER me ayt)

to spread throughout; to get into everything *(verb)*

PERMittEd TO infiltrATE

The word *permeate* combines the Latin prefix per- (meaning "through") with the verb *meare*, meaning "to pass." Thus, something that *permeates* is something that passes through.

pervasive (per VAY siv)

having the quality to be everywhere at the same time *(adjective)*

PERFUME INVADES EVERYTHING

The verb form of pervasive, *pervade* combines the Latin prefix per- (meaning "through") and the Latin verb *vádere* (meaning "to go"). Similar words include *invade* (literally "to go in") and *evade* ("to go away from").

ponderous (PON dur us)

unwieldy from weight or bulk; boring *(adjective)*

HIPPOPOTAMUS

The word *ponderous* derives from the Latin word meaning "weight." This makes sense, since something that is *ponderous* is very weighty.

remote (ri MOAT)

slight; located far away *(adjective)*

THREE VOTES

The word *remote* shares a Latin root with *remove*. This makes sense, since something that is *remote* has been *removed* to a distant location.

replete (ruh PLEET)

full; abundantly supplied *(adjective)*

I EAT AND EAT 'TIL I'M REPLETE

The Latin word *plere*, meaning "to fill," is the root of *replete* (literally "to refill"), *deplete* ("to un-fill"), and *complete* (literally "filled with").

sedentary (seh dun TEH ree)

settled; tending toward inaction *(adjective)*

DEAD AND BURIED

The word *sedentary* comes from the Latin word meaning "to sit." Other words sharing this root include *sediment* (stuff that settles at the bottom of a liquid) and *seance* (at which people sit down to commune with the spirit world).

transitory (TRAN sih tor ee)

short-lived or temporary *(adjective)*

TRANSIT STORY

Like other words that begin with transit- (*transition, transitional, transitive*), *transitory* is used to describe something that is in the process of changing. In the movie *Planes, Trains, and Automobiles*, Steve Martin had a *transitory* relationship with John Candy.

truncated (TRUNG kay tid)

shortened or cut off *(adjective)*

 TRUNK ABBREVIATED

The word *truncate* derives from the Latin word meaning "to cut." In English, the word implies the act of cutting. A *truncated* conversation, for example, is not merely brief. Rather, it has been cut short by one of the participants.

DRILLS

I. Match the word in the left-hand column with the word or phrase in the right-hand column that is most similar in meaning.

1. burgeoning		a.	large and heavy
2. capacious		b.	truncated
3. curtailed		c.	outdated
4. permeating		d.	habitual
5. ponderous		e.	roomy
6. remote		f.	pervasive
7. replete		g.	motionless
8. sedentary		h.	full
9. archaic		i.	new
10. inveterate		j.	distant
11. novel		k.	growing quickly

II. Choose the word that best completes the sentences.

12. "Bill goes to sleep by 9 p.m. every night. He's hardly what I'd call _____."
    a. timid
    b. nocturnal
    c. soporific
    d. surreptitious

13. "My teenage child is totally obnoxious, but fortunately adolescence is a _____ phase, not a permanent one."
    a. transitory
    b. capacious
    c. burgeoning
    d. nocturnal

14. "I can't understand why the jury found the defendant 'not guilty.' I was convinced that the prosecutor had _____ evidence."

    a. debunked
    b. ample
    c. dubious
    d. prosaic

15. "I can't come to visit you anymore, because the _____ amount of cat dander in your house aggravates my allergies."

    a. copious
    b. pitiful
    c. minuscule
    d. archaic

16. "The young children feared the elephant at the circus because it is such a _____."

    a. harbinger
    b. novice
    c. behemoth
    d. burgeon

SAY WHAT?

Words Relating to How Well You Understand

ambiguous (am BIG yoo us)

unclear; open to more than one interpretation *(adjective)*

I AM BIG-TIME CONFUSED

The word *ambiguous* combines the Latin root ambi–, meaning "around," and the verb *agere*, which means "to drive." Literally, the word means "to drive around." An *ambiguous* message avoids (or "drives around") clear meaning, leaving its meaning unclear.

clarity (KLAR ih tee)

clearness, either in appearance or in thought and expression *(noun)*

THE SECRET TO MY CLEAR TEA, IS TO NEVER LET THE BAG TOUCH THE WATER!

CLEAR TEA

The word *clarity* derives from the Latin word *clarus*, meaning "clear." Other words with the same root include *clairvoyant* (one who can see the future clearly), *clarion* (an adjective meaning "clear"), and *declare*.

cogent (KO jent)

logical and convincing *(adjective)*

COnvincing GENT

To say something is *cogent* is a powerful compliment because it implies that something is both true and persuasive. In contrast, textbooks contain lots of truths but they aren't usually very interesting; a demagogue might be persuasive but not truthful. To say an argument, term paper, etc., is *cogent* is to praise it highly.

convoluted (kon vo LOO tid)

intricate; complex; having numerous overlapping coils or spirals *(adjective)*

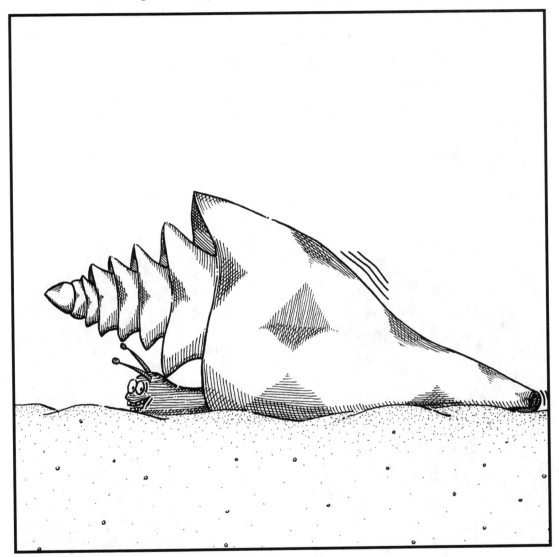

 A **CON**CH HAS A **VOLUTE** SHELL

A *volute* is a spiral or scroll-shaped form. In its most common usage, *convoluted* describes things that are unnecessarily complicated, such as *convoluted* reasoning or a *convoluted* explanation.

incisive (in SYE siv)

cutting; clear, sharp, and penetrating, as a comment or observation *(adjective)*

 INCISOR

A good synonym for *incisive* is trenchant. Both words are used to describe comments and observations that cut through the hogwash and get directly to the heart of the matter.

intuitive (in TOO ih tiv)

knowing or perceiving quickly and readily by intuition *(adjective)*

 INTUITion LIVEs IN HER!

The word *intuitive* is used to describe intelligence that is not learned. *Intuitive* knowledge is apparently natural and instinctive.

naive (na EEV)

lacking sophistication; innocent, like a child *(adjective)*

NAh, I'VE NEVER HEARD OF IT

The word *naive* comes from the Latin word meaning "native." The word was used specifically to describe a person who lived outside the city; it implied that the person was uncultured and unsophisticated.

novice (NAH vis)

beginner (noun)

The word *novice* derives from the Latin word *novus*, meaning "new." Other words sharing this root are *renovate*, *innovate*, *novel*, and *novelty*.

obscure (ob SKYOOR)

dark; not clear or easily understood *(adjective)*

OBSTRUCT YOUR VISION

The word *obscure* has numerous definitions, especially as an adjective. It can mean "dark" (an *obscure* alley), "unknown" (an *obscure* poet), "difficult to understand" (an *obscure* philosophy), or "inconspicuous" (an *obscure* flaw).

quandary (KWAN dree)

a state of uncertainty or perplexity (noun)

QUITE WANDER-Y

Synonyms for *quandary* include predicament, dilemma, and imbroglio. Someone in a *quandary* can be described as nonplused (meaning "befuddled; at a loss for what to say or do").

specious (SPEE shus)

appearing to be true, but actually false *(adjective)*

SPEeCh Is bOgUS

An important distinction between a *specious* argument and a spurious argument is that the former appears to be true but disintegrates upon consideration; the latter is simply false.

spurious (SPYOOR ee us)

not genuine; fake *(adjective)*

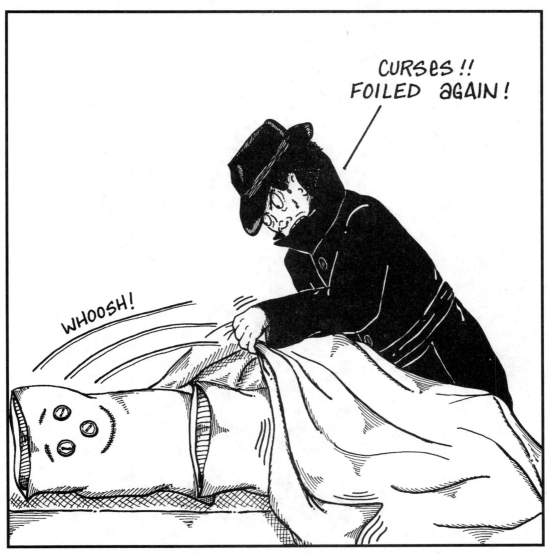

 SPy IS FURIOUS

The spy pictured above is furious because he's been fooled by a *spurious* clue. The word *spurious* derives from the Latin word meaning "illegitimate." One of the lesser-used meanings of *spurious* is "of illegitimate birth." Therefore, it would be redundant to call someone a *spurious* bastard.

stupor (STOO puhr)

a state of reduced or suspended ability *(noun)*

 STUpid from PORt wine

The word *stupor* is often associated with alcohol. A person who has drunk too much is often described as being in a drunken *stupor*.

stymie (STY mee)

stump; thwart; block *(verb)*

 BLIMEY

In golf, a *stymie* occurs when one player's ball is between another player's ball and the hole on the putting green. When this occurs, the player who is closer to the hole replaces his ball with an unobtrusive marker.

vacuous (VAK yoo us)

empty; stupid *(adjective)*

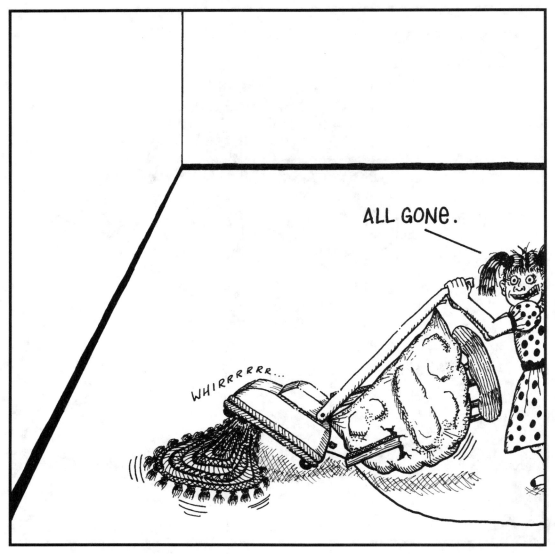

VACUum OUt + S

An empty space can be described as *vacuous*, but the word is most often used to describe someone whose brain is empty. Such a person might be described as a *vacuous* airhead.

DRILLS

CHAPTER 16

I. Match the word in the left-hand column with the word or phrase in the right-hand column that is most similar in meaning.

1. ambiguous		a. plausible but incorrect
2. stymied		b. beginner
3. specious		c. false
4. spurious		d. empty
5. cogent		e. unclear
6. vacuous		f. gullible
7. convoluted		g. convincing
8. novice		h. complicated
9. naive		i. confused

II. Choose the word that best completes the meaning of the sentence.

10. "Is your decision based on facts and careful consideration, or is it merely _____?"
   a. intuitive
   b. dilatory
   c. furtive
   d. boisterous

11. "Our view of the sunset was _____ by the tall buildings."
   a. annihilated
   b. mollified
   c. curtailed
   d. obscured

III. **Complete the story by choosing the correct words from the box.**

"On the night of his twenty-first birthday, my friend Bill did something really stupid. He went to a bar and drank himself into a _____ . His
12.

thinking was very muddleheaded, no _____ to it whatsoever. That
13.

left us, his friends, in quite a _____ ; Bill wanted to drive home even
14.

though he was too drunk to drive. It took a long time and a lot of effort to

finally get his keys away from him."

IT'S TRICKY:

Words Relating to Degrees of Difficulty

abstruse (ab STROOS)

difficult to understand *(adjective)*

 I'M ABSolutely TRUly confuSEd

The word *abstruse* is most often used to describe the complex ideas of scientists, mathematicians, and scholars. The word implies that these ideas are too difficult for us "mere mortals" to understand.

arduous (AR joo us)

difficult; requiring a great deal of hard work *(adjective)*

THIS IS HARD TO US!

The word *arduous* is typically used to describe a task that requires hard work over a long period of time, such as an "arduous cross-country journey" or an "arduous ascent of Mount Everest."

auspicious (aw SPISH us)

suggesting in advance the likelihood of success or good fortune *(adjective)*

A WISH FOR US

The word *auspicious* usually describes something in its beginning stages. A new singer or actor is said to have made an *auspicious* debut if his or her first work shows great promise; a store that sells out its stock in its first day of business has had an *auspicious* opening.

dogged (DAW gid)

stubbornly persevering *(adjective)*

DOG SLED

The word *dogged* takes its meaning from the verb form of *dog*, which means "to pursue with great persistence." Someone who is *dogging* you is *dogged* in his pursuit.

facile (FA sil)

achieved with little effort; easy *(adjective)*

FAT SMILE

The word *facile* has both positive and negative connotations. It can describe something done with effortless grace and ease; it can also be used to describe an idea that is superficial and shallow. Stealing candy from a baby is a *facile* move; you may even see a "fat smile" on the perpetrator's face.

futile (FYOOT uhl)

having no significant result; foolish *(adjective)*

TOO FEW TILES

The word *futile* derives from the Latin word *futilis*, which the ancient Romans used to describe a leaky jug or vase. This makes sense, since it is *futile* to try to carry water in a leaky jug!

immutable (ih MYOO tuh bul)

not able to be changed; stable (adjective)

I'M U TABLE

The Latin word *mutare* means "to change." Something that is *immutable* cannot be changed. The word *mutare* is also the root of the English words *mutate*, *mutation*, and *permutation*.

impenetrable (im PEN ih truh bul)

impossible to enter; incapable of being understood *(adjective)*

 IMPOSSIBLE TO PENETRATE

Synonyms for *impenetrable* include impassable, unnavigable, impermeable, and impregnable.

tenacity (tuh NAS ih tee)

persistence in maintaining or adhering to something valued or habitual *(noun)*

TENNIS ACE+ITY

Someone who demonstrates great *tenacity* is said to be *tenacious*, such as the determined tennis player in the illustration above.

DRILLS

II. **Choose the word or pair of words that best completes the meaning of the sentence.**

1. Although the assignment required _____ efforts on the part of most students, Helene, a _____ student, quickly finished it with little difficulty.
   a. facetious – didactic
   b. arduous – facile
   c. rancorous – frenetic
   d. pervasive – sedentary

2. The pitcher Kerry Wood had an _____ rookie year, winning many games and striking out an impressive number of batters.
   a. auspicious
   b. portentous
   c. nocturnal
   d. insipid

3. The laws of man may change, but the laws of God are _____.
   a. deleterious
   b. itinerant
   c. arid
   d. immutable

4. According to legend, the ancient castle of Dunsinoor was _____; the legend arose from the fact that no entrances could be seen on its walls, and no one was ever seen entering or exiting the castle.
   a. timorous
   b. impenetrable
   c. intrepid
   d. feral

5. Despite the Mounties' _____ pursuit of the criminal, the chase proved _____, as the fugitive eluded the Canadian police.
   a. emphatic - garrulous
   b. penitent - omnipotent
   c. dogged - futile
   d. benign - soporific

6. The mathematics grad student tackled the difficult proof with great _____ and, because of his diligent efforts, eventually solved the _____ problem.
   a. affability - reticent
   b. tenacity - abstruse
   c. stupor - opulent
   d. torpor - cantankerous

CHAPTER **18**

PUZZLES

WORD SEARCH 1

The answers to all of the clues below are hidden in the letter diagram. Answers can all be found in a straight line, either forwards, backwards, up, down, or diagonally. As an extra hint, the clues are listed in alphabetical order of the answers.

```
P S A S S U O I T I T P E R R U S
A R U U U L O R P R E C E P T E U
R P L O O M A W R Y N O E G R U B
S U O N I E H N O E K A T E E N S
I N V E R T A L D E B U N K U F T
M C A G U R N U I E V E T U Q E A
O T U I P G R E G A R I O U S T N
N I S D S P E V I S U F F E U T T
I L T N S U O R O C E D E A R E I
O I E I T R O P U T S S E L B R A
U O R N A I V E S P E N I T E N T
S U E V I S A V R E P N O V I C E
J S T R A T A G E M Y F I C A P D
```

1. AUNT STERNEST _____

2. BRUSH OFF THE QUESTION _____

3. BURGERS, ONE AFTER THE OTHER _____

4. CONSCIENCE SENT US _____

5. DE (AS IN "UN")BUNK _____

6. DECENT AND COURTEOUS _____

7. HE FUSSES VERY MUCH _____

8. GREET, GAB, AND TELL RIOTOUS STORIES _____

9. HE IS NOT JUST _____

10. JUSTICE RISES UP FROM RULES AND EVIDENCE _____

11. NAH, I'VE NEVER HEARD OF IT _____

12. NO ADVICE, BECUSE A NOVICE IS NEW TO HIS JOB _____

13. PEACE-IFY _____

14. PAUPER'S IN THE MONEY _____

15. PENITENTIARY _____

16. PERFUME INVADES EVERYTHING _____

17. PREACHING ACCEPTED _____

18. PRODUCES BIG 'UNS _____

29. PUNCTUAL IS US _____

20. PURE, IS IT? _____

21. SEA OF GREEN _____

22. SLING DIRT _____

23. SPY IS FURIOUS _____

24. SET A TRAP THAT GETS THEM _____

25. STUPID FROM PORT WINE _____

26. SUBSTANCE IS VALIDATED _____

27. SURPRISE LIKE A REPTILE (+TIOUS) _____

28. RUN BETTER _____

29. WITTY AND DRY _____

WORD SEARCH 2

The answers to all of the clues below are hidden in the letter diagram. Answers can all be found in a straight line, either forwards, backwards, up, down, or diagonally. As an extra hint, the clues are listed in alphabetical order of the answers.

```
M F A S T I D I O U S P R U S U I N G
I P R E G N I B R A H D E F U N C T O
L E E D S O S A N B A N K S C P O H T
K A T J U M P L O H O E F O R A G E N
T B A T O L A N I O M T R E P L E T E
N E N N I R R A T R N R A T T A N A L
E R R E C L A M A T I O N E X T T R O
B R O L A S T T D G P P K O N A D E V
M A C U P L E C I T O P S E D B I T E
U T O P A H W B P V T C A V I L R E N
C I N O C A L A E D E P M I P E O V E
N O L A R E F T R U N C A T E D L N B
I N C I S I V E T Y T E L I T U F I T
```

1. A VERY RARE VARIATION _____

2. ABSOLUTELY HORRIBLE _____

3. BEN IS NEVER VIOLENT _____

4. THE CAP IS TOO SPACIOUS _____

5. CALL IT VILE _____

6. CONVINCING GENT _____

7. DE-FUNKED _____

8. DESPICABLE POLITICS _____

9. DISTINCT AND SEPARATE _____

10. FUSSY, TIDY, TEDIOUS _____

11. FERRET WILL SCARE ALL _____

12. FLOWERY RIDDLE _____

13. THANK FRANK FOR HIS HONESTY _____

14. TOO FEW TILES _____

15. HARBOR RINGER MEANS DANGER _____

16. LIMP KNEED _____

17. INCISOR _____

18. ENCOURAGED TO BE HORRIBLE _____

19. INCOME, BECAUSE OF THE RENT _____

20. INVARIABLE, ETERNAL TERRIER _____

21. LACK SONICS _____

22. MILK MONEY _____

23. I'M IMPORTANT _____

24. TOP PERCENT OF EARNERS _____

25. ORNAMENTS BY THE CRATE _____

26. PREJUDICED ORATORY + IVE _____

27. REPORT THE END _____

28. RECLAIM A NATION _____

29. I EAT AND EAT 'TIL I'M _____

30. TEMPERATURE IS MIDDLING _____

31. RAPID PALPITATION _____

32. TRUNK ABBREVIATED _____

33. UN + PAL-ABLE _____

34. USE YOUR POWER _____

35. WORRY AND SCARY _____

CROSSWORD 1

ACROSS

1. GEE! LOWER YOUR BROW!

5. POINT OF A ROMANTIC NOVEL

7. IT'S CLEAN

8. COST IN YOUR FACE (+ IOUS)

13. TINY VERSE

15. CONTROVERSIAL FLAG ACTION

17. THIS TIP IS BETWEEN THE TWO OF US

19. MEGA-PARTICULAR + OUS

20. FACE TIPS YOU OFF + S

21. THE FEAST IS POSSIBLE

DOWN

2. THE WATERS __/DOWN THE DRAIN
3. COMPANY TELLING EMPLOYEE
4. BIGOTED HAYSEED
6. A WISH FOR US
7. PLAYS I'VE WRITTEN
9. IMPULSE PROMPTS YOU
10. STONY AND ICY
11. TRANSIT STORY
12. I'M U TABLE
14. INNER FATE
16. CAUSE HYSTERICS
18. PAINT YOUR WALL

CROSSWORD 2

ACROSS

1. CLEAR TEA

4. FAT SMILE

6. TEMPERATURE IS GREAT

9. MON AMI OR AMIGO

12. CONTAINS "IDLE"

15. MINOR CONSEQUENCES

16. CONTROVERSIAL TO CONTRADICT

18. WISH LIST-LESS

19. AD MAN'S RANT IS FORCEFUL

21. STRAIT-LACED

22. COMRADES, YOU AND ME

DOWN

1. RANT HIS ANGER AT US
2. APPROPRIATE
3. VACUUM OUT + S
5. LIE IN A TABLOID
7. SEE JULIE DANCE
8. A PUG NAMED VICIOUS
10. IMPOSSIBLE TO PENETRATE
11. EMOTIONAL LINIMENT
13. EMBROIDER, WITH RELISH
14. RULES ABUSED
17. TORPEDOED VIGOR
20. AREA RID OF WATER

CROSSWORD 3

ACROSS

1. FULL OF MENACE

5. THIS IS HARD TO US!

7. TACK IT SHUT

10. 'DIS AIN'T A GENUINE RESPONSE

12. CLOAK AND DAGGER

14. LITTLE INJURIES, ENORMOUS LAWSUITS

16. A CONCH HAS A VOLUTE SHELL

17. INTUITION LIVES IN HER

18. I'M ABSOLUTELY TRULY CONFUSED

19. DUPE US

DOWN

2. FROM MERCIFUL TO FURIOUS

3. EX-CULPRIT

4. INTRIGUED BY PITFALLS

6. DIS + SPAR + RAGE

8. MATT IS ALWAYS VIOLENT

9. SUPER FLUSH

10. DICTATOR'S STYLE

11. SUPPER WAS TERRIFIC

13. SOLVES THE RENT PROBLEM

15. MIX THE LETTERS OF MELODY TO (ALMOST) GET __

WORD SCRAMBLE 1

We've scrambled thirty of the Key Words into the nonsense phrases on the next page. Unscramble the words and match them up with the clues, writing the words in the spaces provided. As an extra hint, the clues are listed in alphabetical order of the Key Words.

1. ANT HILL I ATE _____

2. ASS IN THE DUST _____

3. BIG, HEAVY MOTHER _____

4. "YOU CAN'T MAKE US!" _____

5. WELL, IT'S SERIOUS _____

6. DID ACT LIKE A TEACHER _____

7. DIFFICULTY BEING CONFIDENT _____

8. BEING TOO __/CAN KILL A GENT _____

9. DISSATISFIED STUDENT _____

10. EGG REGIS _____

11. DEGENERATE _____

12. EXAMPLE + STAR _____

13. FRACAS _____

14. GABBY, RUDE, LOUD + S _____

15. IMPERIAL LOUSE _____

16. IMPOSSIBLE TO MAKE PEACEABLE _____

17. IRATE AND UNSOCIABLE _____

18. ITINERARY MAN _____

19. CLOCK SPURNER AL _____

20. OBSTINATE FOR THE DURATION _____

21. PARTY'S MAN _____

22. PLENTY POSSIBLE _____

23. PROPHET-LIKE _____

24. QUITE WANDER-Y, AS IF YOU WERE LOST _____

25. REPLIES ARE TOO CLEVER! _____

26. RETIRING + SILENT _____

27. SHE SANG WE WILL WIN _____

28. A SONG FOR US _____

29. SUB + PRESS _____

30. TIMID IN THE CHORUS _____

AIR PANTS

BAIL CRIES

BEARD OUT

BETH HOME

BULLIES PA

CAMP I LABEL

CORN NUT AL

DARN QUAY

DID CACTI

DID IN SETS

EERIEST LOUD

GEORGIE'S U

GLIDE TIN

HAIL AT NINE

IF CARS OUT

IF FIND TED

I'M SOUPIER

INANE GUS

INERT ETC

M ACCOUNT IOUS

NEVER EAT

NITE TRAIN

PEAR TREE

PITCH ROPE

PRESS UPS

REPEL MAX

SAL OR GURU

SID U. SOUSA

SOUR SOON

SUIT ROOM

WORD SCRAMBLE 2

We've scrambled thirty of the Key Words into the nonsense phrases on the next page. Unscramble the words and match them up with the clues, writing the words in the spaces provided. As an extra hint, the clues are listed in alphabetical order of the Key Words.

1. ABANDON THE DICTATORSHIP _____

2. RELIEVE THE ACHE _____

3. I AM BIG-TIME CONFUSED _____

4. AMENDABLE _____

5. BEAMING TERRIFICALLY _____

6. CLOSED TO OUTSIDERS _____

7. COHORT + ADHESIVE TAPE _____

8. THE LATE TORY _____

9. SELECT AND PICK _____

10. EMPHASIZE TWICE _____

11. EPISODE ISN'T PHONY _____

12. FABRIC DATE _____

13. FRENZIED + HECTIC _____

14. THAT HACK NEEDS NEEDS SOME NEW IDEAS _____

15. IMPULSE GETS TO US _____

16. UN-NOXIOUS _____

17. INSULTING GENT _____

18. APPLAUD A STORY _____

19. NOT GLORIOUS _____

20. OBSTRUCTING THE GATE _____

21. PERMITTED TO MERGE AND INFILTRATE _____

22. PRACTICAL, NOT ROMANTIC _____

23. PROPER IN SOCIETY _____

24. ANGER PLUS _____

25. REPULSIVE PUG _____

26. SANTA ACTIONS _____

27. DEAD AND BURIED _____

28. SPEECH IS BOGUS _____

29. TENNIS ACE + ITY _____

30. WIN THE CASE _____

ARM CAT, PIG

BAIT FACER

BEAT ACID

BOAT STEIN

C CELTIC E

CHEEKY DAN

CITE A FIB

COAST INN

FIRE CENT

I CAN'T YET

I GO BUM USA

I SOUR TOON

ICES SOUP

IT CAVED IN

LEAN BEAM

LEAVE TAIL

LOST RICE

NEEDS A TRY

NOSE LINT

PIE MATCH

PINY HEAP

PIOUS MUTE

PRIOR TYPE

RAM TEPEE

ROUT A LADY

SHOE VICE

SOUR ACORN

TARDY OIL

TAP GUNNER

UNO COUSIN

Cross-Out 1

Twenty Key Words are hidden to the right of each of the clues below. To find the Key Word on each line, cross out the number of letters indicated at the end of each clue. As an extra hint, the clues are listed in alphabetical order of the Key Words.

Example: ABSOLUTELY HORRIBLE (4) T̶R̶ A B T̶ H O R T̶

1. DAD THE SAGE (5) F A N D O A L G E T

2. I AM PLENTY BIG (5) T R A M A P O L E Y

3. ARCHAEOLOGICAL RELIC (4) B A R O C H A R I C E

4. BROKEN LITTLE OLD MAN (6) H Y B R I D E T O T A L E

5. COPIER GOES NUTS (6) C O M P L A I N O T U S K

6. THE MOUSE HAS A CURT TAIL (6) C H O U F I R T A Z I L P

7. DOG SLED (4) D R O P G A G E N D

8. ENEMY MIGHTY ANGRY (6) F R I E N D S M I T T Y

9. FLOW LIKE LIQUID (4) F A L P U R I D E

10. HEATHENS REALLY SAY THESE THINGS (4) C H E F O R E S A Y

11. AIN'T GRATEFUL (5) T I N G O R M A T R E L

12. CAMP TUNE (4) G L A M I S P O O N S

13. NEW SCENT (5) N A P O S A C K E N O T

14. BOMB IN THE HOUSE (5) D O R M I T N O R U S H

15. SAUCE PITY (7) P L A Y U P E C H I T Y P E

16. PROSE + ICK! (4) S P I R O S A T T I C

17. THREE VOTES (5) R E D S M O K I T E M

18. BLIMEY (4) S T A Y O N M I C E

19. IT MADE TODD SICK (6) S T R O N G O X I C O

20. VILLAIN-IFY (4) V A I N C L I F F Y

CROSS-OUT 2

Twenty Key Words are hidden to the right of each of the clues below. To find the Key Word on each line, cross out the number of letters indicated at the end of each clue. As an extra hint, the clues are listed in alphabetical order of the Key Words.

Example: ABSOLUTELY HORRIBLE (4) T̶R̶A B T̶H O R T̶

1. ADDS WITH LIBERTY (4)   G R A D O L I M B
2. APPROPRIATE WORDS (5)   T A P E R O M P R O S E
3. BE NICE (4)   B E G O N E S I G N
4. CAN STAND ON HIS WORD (5)   C L A N K I D I O R Y
5. CORD + DIAL (5)   C H O I R E D I P A L E
6. D GRADE (5)   F A D E G R E E M A D E
7. I DOUBT IT, IT'S BOGUS (6)   D R U M B L I P O P U S E
8. FAR FETCHED (4)   O F C A U R C E R
9. FUR-GITIVE (4)   F O U R S T R I V E R
10. IDEAL-LIKE (6)   K I D D Y B E L L T I C K
11. IN YOU SIP, THEN SPIT (5)   W I N S C R I P L I D S
12. MAD ALICE MAKES LICE (5)   S M A L L M I C K E Y
13. NOVELTY STORE (4)   S N O W E V E L T
14. PANDA STANDER (4)   S P A I N R I D E R
15. PICTURE OF JUSTICE (4)   P I L O T F U S E
16. RAPPER AND HIS COHORT (4)   T R A P S P O P A R T
17. SQUASH + SLOBBER (5)   B I S Q U E V A L O R E
18. THE WART (5)   S T A S H W E A R T H
19. URBAN-Y (4)   C U R E B E A N E Y
20. ZESTY FELLAS (4)   Z E B R A B L O U S E

CROSS-OUT 3

Twenty Key Words are hidden to the right of each of the clues below. To find the Key Word on each line, cross out the number of letters indicated at the end of each clue. As an extra hint, the clues are listed in alphabetical order of the Key Words.

Example: ABSOLUTELY HORRIBLE (4) T̸R̸A B T̸H O R T̸

1. AFFECTION-ABLE (4) S C A R F F T A B L E
2. ARGUMENT BISECTOR (4) C A R B R I N T E R M
3. BOMB BLAST OF WORDS (5) B O R E D I M B O A S T
4. CAPTAIN'S LOG (4) C A N T G O A L O N G
5. COOK UP A PLAN (4) S C O U R M O P
6. DISSING AND DARING (5) D R A I N S D A R I N D
7. EMU I'LL IMITATE (4) K E M P U P L A T E R
8. FEVER BURNS WHILE YOU SHIVER (4) C A F E B R O I L E R
9. HIGH AND MIGHTY (5) P H A T R O U G H T O Y
10. THE IMP INFRINGES WHERE HE DOESN'T BELONG (5)
                         R I M S P R I N G O E R
11. LAME END (4) B L A M E K N O T S
12. MAKE OLLIE FINE (4) M O L D F L I P F R Y
13. OBSTRUCT YOUR VISION (4) B O B S A C O U R S E
14. PARROTY-Y COMEDY (4) P L A Y R O D E Y O
15. HIPPOPOTAMUS (5) U P O N A D E E R M O U S E
16. PROUD STUDENT (5) P A R K R U D E N O T E
17. REVEAL RESPECT (4) F O R E V E R B E N
18. TENSE AND NERVOUS (5) S T E R N D U O R U S H
19. TRIVIAL AND TEDIOUS (5) T H R I L L A T E N
20. WILL BE SLY (4) T W I C E F L Y

CHAPTER 19

PUZZLE ANSWERS

WORD SEARCH 1 ANSWERS

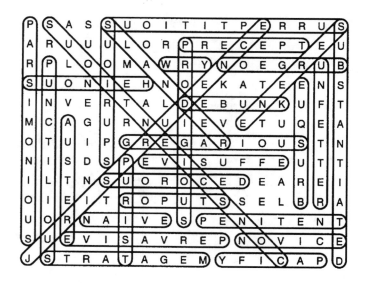

1. AUNT STERNEST _AUSTERE_

2. BRUSH OFF THE QUESTION _BRUSQUE_

3. BURGERS, ONE AFTER THE OTHER _BURGEON_

4. CONSCIENCE SENT US _CONSCIENTIOUS_

5. DE (AS IN "UN") BUNK _DEBUNK_

6. DECENT AND COURTEOUS _DECOROUS_

7. HE FUSSES VERY MUCH _EFFUSIVE_

8. GREET, GAB, AND TELL RIOTOUS STORIES _GREGARIOUS_

9. HE IS NOT JUST _HEINOUS_

10. JUSTICE RISES UP FROM RULES AND EVIDENCE _JURISPRUDENCE_

11. NAH, I'VE NEVER HEARD OF IT _NAIVE_

12. NO ADVICE, BECAUSE A NOVICE IS NEW TO HIS JOB _NOVICE_

13. PEACE-IFY _PACIFY_

14. PAUPER'S IN THE MONEY _PARSIMONIOUS_

15. PENITENTIARY _PENITENT_

16. PERFUME INVADES EVERYTHING   <u>PERVASIVE</u>

17. PREACHING ACCEPTED   <u>PRECEPT</u>

18. PRODUCES BIG 'UNS   <u>PRODIGIOUS</u>

19. PUNCTUAL IS US   <u>PUNCTILIOUS</u>

20. PURE, IS IT?   <u>PURIST</u>

21. SEA OF GREEN   <u>SERENE</u>

22. SLING DIRT   <u>SLANDER</u>

23. SPY IS FURIOUS   <u>SPURIOUS</u>

24. SET A TRAP THAT GETS THEM   <u>STRATAGEM</u>

25. STUPID FROM PORT WINE   <u>STUPOR</u>

26. SUBSTANCE IS VALIDATED   <u>SUBSTANTIATED</u>

27. SURPRISE LIKE A REPTILE (+TIOUS)   <u>SURREPTITIOUS</u>

28. RUN BETTER   <u>UNFETTER</u>

29. WITTY AND DRY   <u>WRY</u>

WORD SEARCH 2 ANSWERS

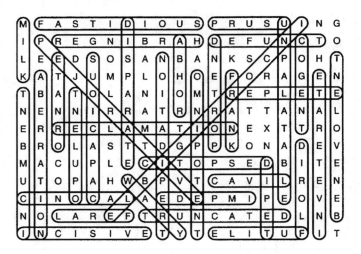

1. A VERY RARE VARIATION <u>ABERRATION</u>

2. ABSOLUTELY HORRIBLE <u>ABHOR</u>

3. BEN IS NEVER VIOLENT (SEE BEN THE HIPPIE) <u>BENEVOLENT</u>

4. THE CAP IS TOO SPACIOUS <u>CAPACIOUS</u>

5. CALL IT VILE <u>CAVIL</u>

6. CONVINCING GENT <u>COGENT</u>

7. DE-FUNKED <u>DEFUNCT</u>

8. DESPICABLE POLITICS <u>DESPOTIC</u>

9. DISTINCT AND SEPARATE <u>DISPARATE</u>

10. FUSSY, TIDY, TEDIOUS <u>FASTIDIOUS</u>

11. FERRET WILL SCARE ALL <u>FERAL</u>

12. FLOWERY RIDDLE <u>FLORID</u>

13. THANK FRANK FOR HIS HONESTY <u>FRANK</u>

14. TOO FEW TILES <u>FUTILE</u>

15. HARBOR RINGER MEANS DANGER <u>HARBINGER</u>

16. LIMP KNEED <u>IMPEDE</u>

17. INCISOR INCISIVE

18. ENCOURAGED TO BE HORRIBLE INCORRIGIBLE

19. INCOME, BECAUSE OF THE RENT INCUMBENT

20. INVARIABLE, ETERNAL TERRIER INVETERATE

21. LACK SONICS LACONIC

22. MILK MONEY MILK

23. I'M IMPORTANT OMNIPOTENT

24. TOP PERCENT OF EARNERS OPULENT

25. ORNAMENTS BY THE CRATE ORNATE

26. PREJUDICED ORATORY + IVE PEJORATIVE

27. REPORT THE END PORTEND

28. RECLAIM A NATION RECLAMATION

29. I EAT AND EAT 'TIL I'M REPLETE

30. TEMPERATURE IS MIDDLING TEPID

31. RAPID PALPITATION TREPIDATION

32. TRUNK ABBREVIATED TRUNCATED

33. UN + PAL-ABLE UNPALATABLE

34. USE YOUR POWER USURP

35. WORRY AND SCARY WARY

CROSSWORD 1 ANSWERS

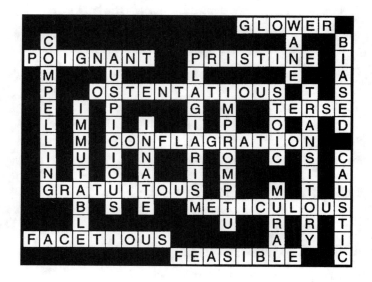

ACROSS

1. GEE! LOWER YOUR BROW! GLOWER

5. POINT OF A ROMANTIC NOVEL POIGNANT

7. IT'S CLEAN PRISTINE

8. COST IN YOUR FACE (+ IOUS) OSTENTATIOUS

13. TINY VERSE TERSE

15. CONTROVERSIAL FLAG ACTION CONFLAGRATION

17. THIS TIP IS BETWEEN THE TWO OF US GRATUITOUS

19. MEGA-PARTICULAR + OUS METICULOUS

20. FACE TIPS YOU OFF + S, PERHAPS WITH A WINK FACETIOUS

21. THE FEAST IS POSSIBLE FEASIBLE

DOWN

2. THE WATERS __/DOWN THE DRAIN   WANE

3. COMPANY TELLING EMPLOYEE   COMPELLING

4. BIGOTED HAYSEED   BIASED

6. A WISH FOR US   AUSPICIOUS

7. PLAYS I'VE WRITTEN   PLAGIARISM

9. IMPULSE PROMPTS YOU   IMPROMPTU

10. STONY AND ICY   STOIC

11. TRANSIT STORY   TRANSITORY

12. I'M U TABLE   IMMUTABLE

14. INNER FATE   INNATE

16. CAUSE HYSTERICS   CAUSTIC

18. PAINT YOUR WALL   MURAL

CROSSWORD 2 ANSWERS

ACROSS

1. CLEAR TEA   CLARITY

4. FAT SMILE   FACILE

6. TEMPERATURE IS GREAT   TEMPERATE

9. MON AMI OR AMIGO   AMIABLE

12. CONTAINS "IDLE"   INDOLENT

15. MINOR CONSEQUENCES   INCONSEQUENTIAL

16. INCONCEIVABLE TO CONTRADICT   INCONTROVERTIBLE

18. WISH LIST-LESS   LISTLESS

19. AD MAN'S RANT IS FORCEFUL   ADAMANT

21. STRAIT-LACED   STAID

22. COMRADES, YOU AND ME   CAMARADERIE

DOWN

1. RANT HIS ANGER AT US   <u>CANTANKEROUS</u>

2. APPROPRIATE   <u>APT</u>

3. VACUUM OUT + S   <u>VACUOUS</u>

5. LIE IN A TABLOID   <u>LIBEL</u>

7. SEE JULIE DANCE   <u>EBULLIENCE</u>

8. A PUG NAMED VICIOUS   <u>PUGNACIOUS</u>

10. IMPOSSIBLE TO PENETRATE   <u>IMPENETRABLE</u>

11. EMOTIONAL LINIMENT   <u>EMOLLIENT</u>

13. EMBROIDER, WITH RELISH   <u>EMBELLISH</u>

14. RULES ABUSED   <u>RUSE</u>

17. TORPEDOED VIGOR   <u>TORPOR</u>

20. AREA RID OF WATER   <u>ARID</u>

CROSSWORD 3 ANSWERS

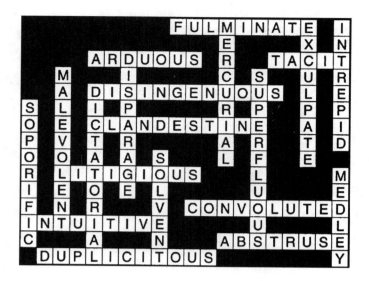

ACROSS

1. FULL OF MENACE   <u>FULMINATE</u>

5. THIS IS HARD TO US!   <u>ARDUOUS</u>

7. TACK IT SHUT   <u>TACIT</u>

10. 'DIS AIN'T A GENUINE RESPONSE   <u>DISINGENUOUS</u>

12. CLOAK AND DAGGER   <u>CLANDESTINE</u>

14. LITTLE INJURIES, ENORMOUS LAWSUITS   <u>LITIGIOUS</u>

16. A CONCH HAS A VOLUTE SHELL   <u>CONVOLUTED</u>

17. INTUITION LIVES IN HER   <u>INTUITIVE</u>

18. I'M ABSOLUTELY TRULY CONFUSED   <u>ABSTRUSE</u>

19. DUPE US   <u>DUPLICITOUS</u>

DOWN

2. FROM MERCIFUL TO FURIOUS <u>MERCURIAL</u>

3. EX-CULPRIT <u>EXCULPATE</u>

4. INTRIGUED BY PITFALLS <u>INTREPID</u>

6. DIS + SPAR + RAGE <u>DISPARAGE</u>

8. MATT IS ALWAYS VIOLENT <u>MALEVOLENT</u>

9. SUPER FLUSH <u>SUPERFLUOUS</u>

10. DICTATOR'S STYLE <u>DICTATORIAL</u>

11. SUPPER WAS TERRIFIC <u>SOPORIFIC</u>

13. SOLVES THE RENT PROBLEM <u>SOLVENT</u>

15. MIX THE LETTERS OF MELODY TO ALMOST GET __ <u>MEDLEY</u>

WORD SCRAMBLE 1 ANSWERS

1. ANT HILL I ATE   <u>ANNIHILATE</u>   HAIL AT NINE
2. ASS IN THE DUST   <u>ASSIDUOUS</u>   SID U. SOUSA
3. BIG, HEAVY MOTHER   <u>BEHEMOTH</u>   BETH HOME
4. "YOU CAN'T MAKE US!"   <u>CONTUMACIOUS</u>   M ACCOUNT IOUS
5. WELL, IT'S SERIOUS   <u>DELETERIOUS</u>   EERIEST LOUD
6. DID ACT LIKE A TEACHER   <u>DIDACTIC</u>   DID CACTI
7. DIFFICULTY BEING CONFIDENT   <u>DIFFIDENT</u>   IF FIND TED
8. BEING TOO __/CAN KILL A GENT   <u>DILIGENT</u>   GLIDE TIN
9. DISSATISFIED STUDENT   <u>DISSIDENT</u>   DID IN SETS
10. EGG REGIS   <u>EGREGIOUS</u>   GEORGIE'S U
11. DEGENERATE   <u>ENERVATE</u>   NEVER EAT
12. EXAMPLE + STAR   <u>EXEMPLAR</u>   REPEL MAX
13. FRACAS   <u>FRACTIOUS</u>   IF CARS OUT
14. GABBY, RUDE, LOUD + S   <u>GARRULOUS</u>   SAL OR GURU
15. IMPERIAL LOUSE   <u>IMPERIOUS</u>   I'M SOUPIER
16. IMPOSSIBLE TO MAKE PEACEABLE   <u>IMPLACABLE</u>   CAMP I LABEL
17. IRATE AND UNSOCIABLE   <u>IRASCIBLE</u>   BAIL CRIES
18. ITINERARY MAN   <u>ITINERANT</u>   NITE TRAIN
19. CLOCK SPURNER AL   <u>NOCTURNAL</u>   CORN NUT AL
20. OBSTINATE FOR THE DURATION   <u>OBDURATE</u>   BEARD OUT
21. PARTY'S MAN   <u>PARTISAN</u>   AIR PANTS
22. PLENTY POSSIBLE   <u>PLAUSIBLE</u>   BULLIES PA
23. PROPHET-LIKE   <u>PROPHETIC</u>   PITCH ROPE
24. QUITE WANDER-Y, AS IF YOU WERE LOST   <u>QUANDARY</u>   DARN QUAY

25.	REPLIES ARE TOO CLEVER!	REPARTEE	PEAR TREE
26.	RETIRING + SILENT	RETICENT	INERT ETC
27.	SHE SANG WE WILL WIN	SANGUINE	INANE GUS
28.	A SONG FOR US	SONOROUS	SOUR SOON
29.	SUB + PRESS	SUPPRESS	PRESS UPS
30.	TIMID IN THE CHORUS	TIMOROUS	SUIT ROOM

WORD SCRAMBLE 2 ANSWERS

1.	ABANDON THE DICTATORSHIP	ABDICATE	BEAT ACID
2.	RELIEVE THE ACHE	ALLEVIATE	LEAVE TAIL
3.	I AM BIG-TIME CONFUSED	AMBIGUOUS	I GO BUM USA
4.	AMENDABLE	AMENABLE	LEAN BEAM
5.	BEAMING TERRIFICALLY	BEATIFIC	CITE A FIB
6.	CLOSED TO OUTSIDERS	CLOISTER	LOST RICE
7.	COHORT + ADHESIVE TAPE	COHESIVE	SHOE VICE
8.	THE LATE TORY	DILATORY	TARDY OIL
9.	SELECT AND PICK	ECLECTIC	C CELTIC E
10.	EMPHASIZE TWICE	EMPHATIC	PIE MATCH
11.	EPISODE ISN'T PHONY	EPIPHANY	PINY HEAP
12.	FABRIC DATE	FABRICATE	BAIT FACER
13.	FRENZIED + HECTIC	FRENETIC	FIRE CENT
14.	THAT HACK NEEDS SOME NEW IDEAS	HACKNEYED	CHEEKY DAN
15.	IMPULSE GETS TO US	IMPETUOUS	PIOUS MUTE
16.	UN-NOXIOUS	INNOCUOUS	UNO COUSIN
17.	INSULTING GENT	INSOLENT	NOSE LINT
18.	APPLAUD A STORY	LAUDATORY	ROUT A LADY
19.	NOT GLORIOUS	NOTORIOUS	I SOUR TOON
20.	OBSTRUCTING THE GATE	OBSTINATE	BOAT STEIN
21.	PERMITTED TO MERGE AND INFILTRATE	PERMEATE	RAM TEPEE
22.	PRACTICAL, NOT ROMANTIC	PRAGMATIC	ARM CAT, PIG
23.	PROPER IN SOCIETY	PROPRIETY	PRIOR TYPE
24.	ANGER PLUS	RANCOROUS	SOUR ACORN

25.	REPULSIVE PUG	REPUGNANT	TAP GUNNER
26.	SANTA ACTIONS	SANCTION	COAST INN
27.	DEAD AND BURIED	SEDENTARY	NEEDS A TRY
28.	SPEECH IS BOGUS	SPECIOUS	ICES SOUP
29.	TENNIS ACE + ITY	TENACITY	I CAN'T YET
30.	WIN THE CASE	VINDICATE	IT CAVED IN

CROSS-OUT 1 ANSWERS

1. DAD THE SAGE (5) ~~F~~ A ~~N~~ D ~~O~~ A ~~L~~ G E ~~T~~
2. I AM PLENTY BIG (5) ~~T~~ ~~R~~ A M ~~A~~ P ~~O~~ L E ~~Y~~
3. ARCHAEOLOGICAL RELIC (4) ~~S~~ A R ~~O~~ C H A ~~R~~ I C ~~E~~
4. BROKEN LITTLE OLD MAN (6) ~~H~~ ~~Y~~ B R I ~~D~~ ~~E~~ T ~~O~~ T ~~A~~ L E
5. COPIER GOES NUTS (6) C O ~~M~~ P ~~L~~ ~~A~~ I ~~N~~ O ~~T~~ U S ~~K~~
6. THE MOUSE HAS A CURT TAIL (6) C ~~H~~ ~~O~~ U ~~F~~ ~~I~~ R T A ~~Z~~ I L ~~P~~
7. DOG SLED (4) D ~~R~~ O ~~P~~ G ~~A~~ G E ~~N~~ D
8. ENEMY MIGHTY ANGRY (6) ~~F~~ ~~R~~ ~~I~~ E N ~~D~~ ~~S~~ M I ~~T~~ T Y
9. FLOW LIKE LIQUID (4) F ~~A~~ L ~~P~~ U ~~R~~ I D ~~E~~
10. HEATHENS REALLY SAY THESE THINGS (4) ~~C~~ H E ~~F~~ ~~O~~ R E S ~~A~~ Y
11. AIN'T GRATEFUL (5) ~~T~~ I N G ~~O~~ R ~~M~~ A T ~~R~~ E ~~L~~
12. CAMP TUNE (4) ~~C~~ L A M ~~I~~ ~~S~~ P O O N ~~S~~
13. NEW SCENT (5) N A ~~P~~ ~~O~~ S ~~A~~ C ~~K~~ E N ~~O~~ T
14. BOMB IN THE HOUSE (5) ~~D~~ O ~~R~~ M I ~~T~~ N O ~~R~~ U S ~~H~~
15. SAUCE PITY (7) P ~~L~~ A ~~Y~~ U ~~P~~ ~~E~~ C ~~H~~ I T Y ~~P~~ ~~E~~
16. PROSE + ICK! (4) ~~S~~ P ~~I~~ R O S A ~~T~~ ~~T~~ I C
17. THREE VOTES (5) R E ~~D~~ ~~S~~ M O ~~K~~ ~~I~~ T E ~~M~~
18. BLIMEY (4) S T ~~A~~ Y ~~O~~ ~~N~~ M I ~~C~~ E
19. IT MADE TODD SICK (6) ~~S~~ T ~~R~~ O ~~N~~ ~~G~~ ~~O~~ X I C ~~O~~
20. VILLAIN-IFY (4) V ~~A~~ I ~~N~~ ~~C~~ L I ~~F~~ F Y

CROSS-OUT 2 ANSWERS

1. ADDS WITH LIBERTY (4) ~~G~~RAD~~O~~LIMB
2. APPROPRIATE WORDS (5) ~~T~~APE~~R~~OMP~~R~~OS~~E~~
3. BE NICE (4) BE~~G~~~~O~~NE~~S~~IGN
4. CAN STAND ON HIS WORD (5) CL~~A~~NK~~I~~D~~I~~ORY~~
5. CORD + DIAL (5) CH~~O~~IR~~E~~DIP~~A~~LE~~
6. D GRADE (5) ~~F~~ADEGRE~~E~~~~M~~ADE
7. I DOUBT IT, IT'S BOGUS (6) DR~~U~~MBL~~I~~P~~O~~P~~U~~S~~E~~
8. FAR FETCHED (4) ~~O~~F~~C~~A~~U~~RCER~~
9. FUR-GITIVE (4) F~~O~~URS~~T~~R~~I~~VER~~
10. IDEAL-LIKE (6) K~~I~~D~~D~~YB~~E~~LL~~T~~ICK~~
11. IN YOU SIP, THEN SPIT (5) ~~W~~INSC~~R~~IPL~~I~~DS~~
12. MAD ALICE MAKES LICE (5) ~~S~~MALL~~M~~ICK~~E~~Y~~
13. NOVELTY STORE (4) ~~S~~NOW~~E~~VELT~~
14. PANDA STANDER (4) ~~S~~PA~~I~~NR~~I~~DER
15. PICTURE OF JUSTICE (4) PIL~~O~~TF~~U~~S~~E~~
16. RAPPER AND HIS COHORT (4) ~~T~~RAP~~S~~PO~~P~~ART
17. SQUASH + SLOBBER (5) ~~B~~ISQUE~~Y~~ALOR~~E~~
18. THE WART (5) ~~S~~TA~~S~~HW~~E~~ARTH~~
19. URBAN-Y (4) ~~C~~URE~~B~~EANEY~~
20. ZESTY FELLAS (4) ZEB~~R~~AB~~L~~OUSE~~

CROSS-OUT 3 ANSWERS

1. AFFECTION-ABLE (4) S̶C̶A R̶F F T̶A B L E
2. ARGUMENT BISECTOR (4) C̶A R B̶R̶I N̶T E R M̶
3. BOMB BLAST OF WORDS (5) B O R̶E̶D̶I̶M B O̶A S T
4. CAPTAIN'S LOG (4) C A N̶T G̶O̶A L O N̶G
5. COOK UP A PLAN (4) S̶C O U R̶M̶O̶P
6. DISSING AND DARING (5) D R̶A I N̶S D A R̶I N D̶
7. EMU I'LL IMITATE (4) K̶E M P̶U P̶L A T E R̶
8. FEVER BURNS WHILE YOU SHIVER (4) C̶A̶F E B R O̶I L E R̶
9. HIGH AND MIGHTY (5) P̶H A T̶R̶O̶U G H T O̶Y
10. THE IMP INFRINGES WHERE HE DOESN'T BELONG (5)
    R̶I M S̶P R̶I N G O̶E R̶
11. LAME END (4) B̶L A M E K̶N O̶T S̶
12. MAKE OLLIE FINE (4) M O L D̶F̶L I P̶F R̶Y
13. OBSTRUCT YOUR VISION (4) B̶O B S A̶C O̶U R S̶E
14. PARROTY-Y COMEDY (4) P L̶A Y̶R O D̶E Y O̶
15. HIPPOPOTAMUS (5) U̶P O N A̶D̶E̶E R M̶O U S E̶
16. PROUD STUDENT (5) P A̶R K̶R̶U D E N O̶T E̶
17. REVEAL RESPECT (4) F̶O̶R E V E R B̶E N̶
18. TENSE AND NERVOUS (5) S̶T E R̶N D̶U O R̶U S H̶
19. TRIVIAL AND TEDIOUS (5) T H̶R I L̶L̶A̶T E N̶
20. WILL BE SLY (4) T̶W I C̶E̶F̶L Y

INDEX

ABOUT THE AUTHORS

Tom Meltzer graduated from Columbia University with a degree in English. For the past twelve years he has worked at The Princeton Review, teaching and developing courses, writing test materials, and authoring or co-authoring seven books, including *The Best 311 Colleges* and *Cracking the CLEP*. In addition to writing and teaching, Tom is also a professional musician and songwriter.

Lisa Vingleman studied art in her native Milwaukee. *Illustrated Word Smart* is her first book. The authors are married and live in Queens, New York.

Bestselling *Smart Guides*
for Students and Adults from

Grammar Smart
0-375-76215-9 • $12.00

**Illustrated
Word Smart**
0-375-75189-0 • $12.95

Math Smart
0-375-76216-7 • $12.00

Math Smart II
0-679-78383-0 • $12.00

**Math Smart
for Business**
0-679-77356-8 • $12.00

Negotiate Smart
0-679-77871-3 • $12.00

Reading Smart
0-679-75361-3 • $12.00

Speak Smart
0-679-77868-3 • $10.00

Word Smart
0-375-76218-3 • $12.00

Word Smart II
0-375-76219-1 • $12.00

Word Smart for Business
0-679-78391-1 • $12.00

Writing Smart
0-375-76217-5 • $12.00

AVAILABLE WHEREVER BOOKS ARE SOLD